Praise for *The G...*

"*The Goddess Resolution*, inspired by the insights of spiritual connection to nature, is brought to life by Kate's personal experiences to readdress harmony and provide coping strategies during challenging times. Whether female or male, the pearls of wisdom and practical exercises within this book help provide an opportunity to find an inner sense of spiritual well-being. Delving into this book on an ongoing basis delivers peace and understanding in line with the energy of divinity within us all."

—Mathew Tyler, cocreator of the
Aboriginal Walkabout Oracle Cards

"The powerful guidance Kate shares in *The Goddess Resolution* will be of great service to all those wanting to heal, learn, and grow as they realize their innate wholeness. A naturally gifted writer, Kate is a twenty-first-century literary shaman living a dynamic family life. And, if you are fortunate enough to read this refreshingly practical compendium of esoteric wisdom, you will experience the real magic she has at her fingertips!"

—J. M. Harrison, award-winning
author of *The Soul Whisperer*

"This wonderfully practical book, which seamlessly engages us in the restorative power of nature and our spiritual integrity, brings together stories, ideas, exercises and wisdom from our distant past and from our intuitive drive to do what feels right and brings us peace. Kate marries the myths of goddesses worldwide with our emotional experiences to help us handle our feelings and direct the energy generated more productively. Whether you are looking for an overhaul of your life or need a little reassurance and guidance from time to time, there is something for you here."

—Susie Anthony, creator of
The Super HERO Code Project and community

the
Goddess
Resolution

About the Author

Kate Osborne is a writer, editor, publisher, and digital artist who founded Solarus Ltd., the UK's leading independent producer of oracle card sets. Previously she was the editor in chief of the esoteric magazine *Kindred Spirit*. Her passion for writing, sacred knowledge, and using that knowledge to connect with others started early in life; she won literary awards whilst at school, discovered diverse cultures through extensive travel and immigration across continents, and fulfilled various counselling and mentoring roles. By the time she was in her twenties, she had already visited much of Europe, Australia, New Zealand, the Pacific Islands, Africa, and America, acquiring knowledge, experience, and a thirst for self-exploration, inspired by ancient cultures and their myths.

Kate's early working life was steered by the sudden loss of her first husband. She immersed herself in various industries, including real estate, local government, the chemical industry, and radio advertising. But the pull of the written word and her need to discover and share teachings from across the globe drew her to publishing. It was during her time at *Kindred Spirit* that she met the people who would later become mentors, friends, and clients when she started her own business in 2008. She offered her "big mouth" and "broad shoulders" to those who found the conventional way of getting their work out both daunting and unrewarding. From ghost-writing, editing, web design, and content writing to creating the much-loved oracle decks that Solarus is now known for, Kate is delighted to present *The Goddess Resolution* as her first self-help offering. Kate now lives with her husband and their two teenage children in South Devon, UK, in the market town of Newton Abbot, where she feels most at home nestled between the stunning moors in one direction and the deep blue sea in the other.

www.solarusltd.com
https://www.facebook.com/Solarus-Ltd-370412643090335

First Edition
First Printing, 2022

Book design by Christine Ha
Cover design by Shannon McKuhen
Editing by Holly Vanderhaar
Interior art by Llewellyn Art Department

Llewellyn Publications is a registered trademark of Llewellyn Worldwide Ltd.

Library of Congress Cataloging-in-Publication Data (Pending)
ISBN: 978-0-7387-6334-7

Llewellyn Publications
A Division of Llewellyn Worldwide Ltd.
2143 Wooddale Drive
Woodbury, MN 55125-2989
www.llewellyn.com

Printed in the United States of America

the Goddess Resolution

Kate Osborne

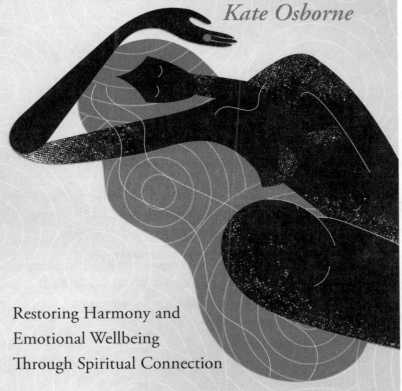

Restoring Harmony and
Emotional Wellbeing
Through Spiritual Connection

Llewellyn Publications | Woodbury, Minnesota

Other Works by Kate Osborne

Dark Goddess Oracle Cards
Witches' Familiars Oracle Cards
Mystic Wanderer Oracle Cards
Aboriginal Walkabout Oracle Cards

Disclaimer

This book and its exercises, rituals, and workings are intended for spiritual and emotional guidance only. They are not intended to replace medical assistance or treatments.

Dedication

For those who resolve to learn from their experiences of this life to achieve a greater sense of peace, or who simply care enough for themselves and others, to reclaim unity of mind, body, and spirit and live a life that is both manageable and fulfilling.

And to my husband Phil, son Kieran, and daughter Shana: you are my most precious teachers, and for all you are, I thank you.

Contents

Exercises

Foreword

Women know how to weave. Since time immemorial, we have sat together to weave not only cloth but the beautiful web of life as we share our stories, wisdom, knowledge, nurturing and our women's magic. My name is Elaina Harvey, and in 1990 I established "Shamanka," now recognised as the only internationally-known school dedicated uniquely to women's shamanism. My medicine name is Shadow Walker, which is where I travel and explore, and my life's work is the quest of the deep, ancient, and potent feminine essence, and to help and support women in this quest, especially in these difficult times. And so it gives me the greatest pleasure to contribute to this remarkable book to aid our journey in these times that are often far detached from our shamanic past.

Contemporary life holds challenges for us; in many cases, we find no answers but may prompt deeper questions about our feelings, reactions, and purpose. The answers may often feel overwhelming, but they can lead us on a quest to find a feminine "Being of Light," one who knows the feminine perspective and our purpose. When we meet them, many of these goddesses may seem to hold reflections of ourselves, giving us visions of our own possibilities of being, seeing, reacting, and choice, including the confidence to take on new challenges, embrace new ways, and say "no." As strong women, we do not need to copy external male attitudes to attain a result.

When we discover the source of any wounding or disempowerment, we can heal and reclaim our core integrity. Practical healing methods are essential, and many can be found in this book, which connects us to ourselves and to nature. The elements play an indispensable role, and as this book demonstrates, the goddesses often are power conduits for our connection to water or fire, for example. A lot of healing and forgiveness may be sought when reclaiming our power to create, and so we turn to the "light": the sacred flame, our passion and our spark.

Here the opportunities exist to explore how we have allowed our flame to be extinguished or dulled by focusing on the negative, as well as revealing our own vital force. In the work I do, this always ends with a "ceremony of Light" in which I use a central altar to hold all of these objects which represent the powers; this is circled with flowers which reveal exquisite beauty and fecundity, for the seeds planted in the womb, container of the feminine principle.

The journey of becoming a "Luminous Warrior" includes the courage to acknowledge our own shadow without beating ourselves up. When we encounter a problem, there is sure to be a goddess who understands us, and who is there to help and bring us insights. This welcome book forms an archive of the profound wisdom and knowledge untapped maybe for many centuries. This work brings a living resource as there are many opportunities to encounter one of these unique beings through ceremony and symbolism, which are clearly explained.

My friend and colleague, Kate Osborne, brings a rich store of deeply studied, researched, explored, and experienced lessons of several goddesses, both well-known and some that many may not have discovered yet. They help us channel the energy we all possess to master our emotions and create a way of living that enriches us and gives us a greater sense of peace and purpose.

—Eliana Harvey, shamanka,
medicine woman, healer, author, and
founder of Shamanka Traditional School
of Women's Shamanism

Introduction

We are all what we believe ourselves to be; as women, we have been told to accept a narrative that has our menfolk often in positions of power "above and beyond" our reach. In reality, this could not be further from the truth. Though people differ physically and chemically, spiritually or energetically we all come from the same source. It is just that over millennia we have been taught to use and express our energy differently. But times are changing, and so are people. New doors and opportunities for self-expression are being revealed, old patterns and dark corners are being exposed, and our emotional intelligence is becoming far more relevant than ever before. And so, regardless of your sex, upbringing, social status, financial position, even societal expectations, you can resolve to do, and be, otherwise, and prosper in ways that can never be lost to you again.

My name is Kate Osborne. I am a mother, wife, and lover of life. And as a former counsellor, now writer, editor, and publisher of esoteric material, I consider myself an exponent of what conventional society refers to as "alternative thinking and practices." This encompasses everything from earth-centred medicine and traditions to realms beyond the here and now. As a woman of both social and intellectual freedom, I have discovered the power of emotional expression. As a person who has suffered great losses, I am learning the skills to harness my emotions for the best outcome possible—a happier, more harmonious, and healthier life. I would like to share all this with you, believing that whatever you face in life, you will cope and gain from it something to restore your harmony and wellbeing.

Getting to Know This Book

The Goddess Resolution looks to de-demonise what is often seen as character faults particular to women, helping us to manage our "energy" better. This energy management and engagement takes shape in practical exercises, meditations, invocations, and anecdotes. This book also guides you a little further down the path of self-discovery and responsibility. The term "goddess" is all-encompassing—much like the word "woman," holding within the masculine version. It does not work the other way around! But the information in this book is not about pitting the masculine and feminine or physical and emotional energies against each other; it is about re-addressing the energetic/emotional balance within us, which then resonates outwards.

The Goddess Resolution sets out to integrate the "universal energy" that is at the heart of everything, sharing your path to a better understanding and development of yourself and the world you create.

With this book, you can engage your emotional self-mastery through the lessons and stories of the "goddess," the creative power that resides in us. This power has been known about since people first walked this earth, and has been tapped into by all peoples from across the globe. This power is universal. It has been interpreted via the myths of "goddesses" from many different cultures, some still living and some now considered ancient or dormant. This book looks to open up the various ways we can connect with this power by revealing and sharing goddesses and practices from a range of cultures and beliefs. In no way is any appropriation or offence intended by so doing.

Along with a diverse range of goddess stories, there is also a wide range of things for you to do, to engage with the natural world, universal energy, and your own power. Some of these might be familiar to you, and others might seem very foreign or unusual. They all come from across the globe, and there are versions of these exercises that appear in various cultures. Again, what is shared with you here are examples that have been shared with me in my travels and taught to me by a variety of wisdom keepers and elders for the benefit of all, regardless of your own belief or cultural identity. It is all stemming from one source, expressed in many ways.

Goddesses and exercises by chapter

"The Power to Create" focuses on what we bring into being. It introduces the stories of Eingana, representing earth-centred traditions, and Lilith, from monastic beliefs, which teach us about manifestation and equality. Exercises include the living breath meditation, creating your own focal point, and walking your own stone spiral.

"The Relationship Ripple" looks at the bonds we form based on our inherent curiosity and/or subsequent need to trust others as we start to construct our world and ourselves. Pandora, representing the direction of the north, and Hine-nui-te-pō, representing the direction of the south, reveal their stories. Exercises to mitigate the fallout of curiosity unchecked and broken trust include a living flame meditation, a self-scrying exercise, a "tipping the bowl" visualisation, and a master weaver visualisation.

"Tackling Temptation" discusses the desire and natural tendency to tempt and persuade others to follow our line of thought. Discover the myth of Deer Woman taking the passive stance, and Uzume, who represents the active role in the lessons of temptation. Exercises include natural grounding, perception practice, and a sun meditation.

"Facing Fallout" looks at how and where this fallout occurs and what we can do to re-address it, starting with ourselves. The goddess energy expressed through the stories of Ran (as a perpetrator) and Sedna (as a victim) deal with some of the darkest consequences of the misuse and imbalance of power. Exercises include creating sacred water, a "dissolution of sorrows" ritual, a "cast in stone" ritual, and calling to the queens.

"Shut Up or Put Up" addresses when we can choose to either be compliant and give in, or to rebel and destroy. The goddess stories of Persephone as the passenger and Kali as the driver are used to demonstrate this. Exercises include the sphere of clarity and the sphere of calm meditations, acknowledging your power visualisation, and sun and moon salutations.

"Becoming the Fortress" introduces Hekate, the triple goddess of protection, exploring what the "triple goddess" aspect means to us all today. Exercises include the circle of protection, the "hailing Hekate" invocation, and the fortress guided visualisation.

"Picking Your Battles" looks at the times when a need for atonement or redemption must be fulfilled. This chapter explores this need and how it can best be managed, even how and when to execute these actions. Skadi, tapping into the element of ice, and Maman Brigitte, harnessing the element of fire, offer compelling depictions of this drive in us. Exercises include a guided journey to the north and a guided journey to the south.

"Death Becomes You" is about coming to terms with radical change: changes in lifestyle, outlook, and fundamental behavioural change, and managing fear. Tlazolteotl (purification) and Oya (deliverance) are goddesses that, at first glance, instill fear of the unknown, of death itself. Still, in resolving to work with these aspects of our lives, they provide an incredible opportunity to rebuild anew. Exercises include hailing the Divine Feminine invocation, experiencing burial in earth, and feeding the earth ritual.

"Born-Again Creators" looks at the importance of making every new beginning count, investing the energy it takes to transform. The story of Gaia provides the inspiration for transformative actions. Exercises include a Gaia attunement and making your own medicine bundle.

Using This Book

It is important to be familiar with the way the exercises, meditations, and so forth work in this book. As a general guide, I would encourage you to read through all the activities before embarking on them. Take your time to find the right locations and gather suitable materials as suggested. Always make this personal to you and do only what feels right for you; this does not always mean "comfortable," because we don't grow or learn by just doing what we have always done. With meditations, it can help to record them too, and then play them back to yourself as you undertake them. Where the exercises call for you to find a place in nature, without suggesting an indoor alternative, then please do make the time to plan for this and do the exercise outside; sometimes, there is no substitute for the healing powers of the great outdoors and our connection to it.

Remember expressing yourself through the landscape of your emotional palette is a natural, healthy, and inherent part of being alive. But when your emotions appear to have a will of their own and control the actions that begin to hamper life or throw you off balance and cause distress and discomfort, it can be immensely helpful to have practical, meaningful steps to redress that. These are not rules or orders that you have to live by; the goddess myths you will learn about in this book embody the energies we must manage and draw upon; they do not pose as matriarchal figures cracking the whip or waving their wand, so to speak. Take from this as much or as little as you feel you need, return to it, use it as a reference for when life throws you a curveball. The resolutions will always be here for you.

Chapter 1
The Power to Create

Y ou are born of a goddess. That is to say, you are born of the most incredible, creative energy known to us today. You are the very stuff of stars that populate the cosmos, with the added ability to make choices about how you wield that creative power. The oldest statues that we have uncovered so far are manifestations of this power, and they take the unmistakable form of goddess idols like the Venus of Hohle Fels (dating back to 38,000 BCE), which supports the veneration of the power of creation long before the Abrahamic religions ever took hold. The way you act and react in life, your emotional response, is the most powerful tool available to you. Mastering your emotions (the most common expression of your "creative energy," also described as your will or spirit) is like finding a unique key. This key can unlock your emotional wellbeing and help you develop a greater understanding and appreciation of how to implement such wisdom in your life today.

When speaking of creation as a concept, most people visualize grand undertakings, often on a biblical scale in which entire worlds come into being. Although creation is seldom so dramatic, it always holds power. Physically, it can manifest in giving birth to another human being, making a home, or preparing a meal. Psychologically, you can create anxiety, fear, or joy. Emotionally, your creative power can determine the mood or atmosphere of any given situation, or affect the way other sentient beings feel around you. Though this may be more challenging as we get older, it is never too late to master. You are your own most significant creation, so that is where the fundamental cornerstones must be most considerately laid down.

What you choose to wear today, how you carry yourself, the mood you are in, what you want to eat, what you say to yourself and others, and how you allow the world around you to impact your being is all creating that very same world around you. And the best part of it is that every day that you wake, you get another opportunity to improve upon, change, or add to this world. You can choose to do or say something neutral or positive, or you can choose to create drama with words and deeds, be thoughtless with your actions, make trouble, or ignore opportunities to change something for the positive. You can let your emotions overrun your life, or you can take control and bring forth a better experience of this life.

The Snake Goddesses

It is no coincidence that the first goddesses revealed to you are also associated with the snake—the epitome of creation energy in the animal kingdom. Eingana is revered as the great snake goddess of the Aboriginal Dreamtime, and Lilith, the often controversial first female deity of organised Abrahamic religion. Eingana, the mother, is most often depicted as a gigantic, thick-bodied formidable snake. And occasionally, more creatively, like a chimaera: snake-like below the waist with a woman's bare torso and head. Lilith is most often depicted as a naked, voluptuous, raven-haired, beautiful woman either holding or entwined with a large snake. The idea here of "snake" energy for both these goddesses is far from sinister or destructive, as in the biblical sense, but rather life-renewing and ongoing, shedding what no longer serves to create the new, over and over again.

Snakes can navigate land and water equally well, and this adaptability and equal status is also expressed through the goddesses. What these goddesses also share with "snake" are some of the most appealing and life-sustaining qualities we can hope to adopt, and which are yours for the taking: giving birth; being supple of mind and body; the ability to get around without causing a disturbance; understanding when to "lie low" or when to rise up and be noticed; being able to shed our past and begin anew—to name a few. In other words, all the attributes to create a world in which all things have their rightful place and purpose on equal footing with everything else.

For most people, the thought of regular meditation seems the stuff of distant fantasy. It conjures up misty images of serene monks atop mountains or beautiful white-clad women on deserted beaches with gently lapping waves kissing their feet. But back in the real world, we simply don't have the time for the luxury of "doing nothing" each day. However, if a few minutes, every day dedicated to easing the mind meant a lifetime of less pressure and confusion, less anger and frustration, and improved health and enjoyment, is that not something worth discovering and undertaking? Meditation costs nothing to do, but your life could prove far more costly without it.

◎ CONSCIOUS BREATH MEDITATION

This meditation is a simple method of watching the breath, relaxing the muscles, and improving our circulation (both physically and energetically), with the benefit of also improving our emotional state.

YOU WILL NEED:

* A quiet space where you can lie down undisturbed for fifteen to twenty minutes

Having found your quiet space and made it comfortable for you to lie down on your back, just relax and breathe normally through the nose. Gradually become aware of the incoming and outgoing breath. Sense the breath entering from the nostrils and trace its movement down to the lungs, sensing and even seeing your chest move, and then watch the reverse process from lungs to nostrils as you exhale. Take your time and repeat the conscious observation of the breath at least eight times. If any sound comes, allow it, but pay attention to your breathing. As you watch the breath, it will slow down on its own; this is the magic and beauty of this meditation. If we don't interfere with the breathing, our breath will become more harmonious and effortless.

As the breathing slows down, notice your body "resting" as the muscles relax. Starting from your head and neck, just allow each part of your body to sink into the floor (or bed or couch). With every slow breath in and out now, let the next section of your body relax through the shoulders, arms, hands and fingers, chest, tummy and buttocks, thighs, lower legs, right to the feet and toes. Let everything just rest, and if you feel discomfort along the way in your body, acknowledge it but then let it go and focus again on the breath. Continue to just relax and release the muscles. Breathe and relax into the feeling of calm and peacefulness that will be washing over and through you. Continue to immerse yourself in the space for another few minutes, then slowly but surely remove the focus from the breath and gently rise by sitting up first and then standing up. Now you are ready for goddess inspiration and creation.

Eingana the Master Manifestor

Eingana's story recounts that all people were carried inside her body as she dwelled in the calm waters and the safety of her cave on this earth. One day the first great rain-time descended on the lands, forcing Eingana into action. Rather than get trapped and possibly drown, she decided to rise from the floodwaters and come out of her cave. From this new vantage point, she could see all the lands before her and finally release all the life she held within her: all the animals, children, men, and women. When the floodwaters receded, and after she released her charges to begin their lives on Earth, Eingana went back to her cave.

However, Eingana maintains a bond with all she has birthed in the form of sinew called "toon." This string-like connection is like a great mystical umbilical cord. Eingana keeps hold of that string all the time. When our time on this earth is at an end, it is said Eingana lets that string go (cuts the cord, so to speak), and we die. However, should this great mother of humanity ever be destroyed, everything will cease to be. This possibility is akin to something referred to by the British writer and journalist Graham Hancock as the "Mother" culture, in which cataclysmic events might have destroyed great civilizations, with humanity obliged to begin again with no memory of what went before.

Relating Eingana's creation story to the art of making things happen means we have a responsibility towards the things we create and the people we are connected to, especially when what we create does not always bring the results we desire. For example, how many times have you begun a relationship and created a bond, only to have it break down, to feel disappointment and resentment when once there was so much hope and promise? This breakup may have felt like a cataclysmic event. Still, we can learn to manage our feelings better, see the experience for what it truly is, and move on to form another relationship that has a better chance of lasting. And not just because the next person may be different from the last, but because we have changed too, and have a better understanding of ourselves and how to manage our emotions when things get challenging.

Birthing Your World

Eingana's creative surge may come into your life in a manner very personal to you. Perhaps you will see or sense her in a vision nothing like the traditional images. That is just fine. As you will read in her story, a catalyst prompted her to release her creations, and so too it will be a catalyst in your life, an event, physical or emotional, that will awaken her within yourself. Eingana's actions are related to a great flood, and this idea of a cataclysmic flood is not uncommon in many beliefs and religions. The tidal surges that move the great bodies of water around the world, under the spell of the moon and its gravitational pull, will be like the trigger that releases within you Eingana's presence. A profound stirring of emotions, in either direction, for positive reasons or not, will be what calls her to you. When she appears, snake-like or otherwise, she will say nothing, but rather "birth" all the ideas and possibilities you have been holding within during a dream state. Much like watching a movie, you can expect your thoughts to play out before your eyes, like a stream of trailers for upcoming features. By the time you awaken, one or two will resonate, still evident in the memory, and this will be your cue to act on them; no need to blindly repeat the negative patterns of the past. We can use, rather than lose, our memories of what went before, and use them as building blocks for a better outcome.

And with everything you create, you are always connected to it by a "toon," a strand of your own energy. This strand may be in the form of feelings created by your actions; it may be a bond of blood in terms of family; it may be a spiritual cord, an impact that a situation or a person has had on you, or you have had in reverse. In essence, it can be seen as a sense of responsibility, duty, or custodianship for what you have created. In that sense—like the idea that when Eingana is no more, all she was attached to, responsible for, will cease to be—failing to take responsibility for what and how you create can have destructive consequences. So, bearing that in mind, learning to use your creative power wisely is not only beneficial but essential.

◎ Creating a Focal Point

One of the most practical and simple ways to stimulate and channel your creative power is to connect with the energies all about you, from your past, present, and future, from worlds seen and unseen. Creating and visiting a "focal point" (altar, sacred space, temple, or shrine) that hosts all these elements, and that is personal to you, is the exercise chosen for you to undertake. It will become something you can return to time and time again, as and when you wish, to draw support and creative inspiration or to be with your thoughts.

YOU WILL NEED:

* A small area set aside somewhere quiet, either in your home or garden (depending on your preference); this could be as simple as a window ledge, a corner of a room, space on a bookshelf, the hollow of a tree, or a small stone circle, entirely up to you. But be mindful that it is a place that will remain undisturbed by others or the elements. It will also house trinkets and things of value to you (like photos, precious stones, etc.), so it should not be in a place where it may become a temptation to others.

* A small handheld bell to "clear" or cleanse the space by agitating and moving the energy with sound vibration

* Representations of the elements (earth, air, fire, water). Examples include, for earth: a gnome figurine, a black candle, a pebble or stone; for air: a feather, a white candle, a small bell; for fire: a red candle, a dragon or lizard figurine, a piece of amber; for water: a small bowl of water, moonstone, a blue candle).

* Representations of the ancestors. If this relates to direct relatives, then use either a photo of them or something that connects you to them, like an old ring, watch, scarf, etc., and if this relates to long ago ancestors or deities (either monastic or of the "old" religions), then a little statue or image to represent them will suffice. Something that is representative of you. This could be as abstract as a colour (so something blue or red or green), or even a photo of a child (you as a child or a picture of your child), or something you hold dear.

Walk around the home or garden to get a good feel for where you want to create your focal point. The most important thing is that this space you select is private and quiet, and the "offerings" placed there will remain undisturbed. When you have located the right area, make room, if need be. Wipe surfaces down or, if outside, clear leaves or move any significant protruding matter where possible. The next thing to do is to energetically "clear" the space. Some people may choose to acknowledge the six directions they are about to engage with using an invocation or prayer, but this is not necessary. It is enough to make your intention clear—that what you are about to do is cleanse and balance the energies that come into direct contact with your focal point.

Taking the bell, begin to ring as you move it straight ahead of you—northwards. Then to your right—eastwards, then back to yourself—southwards. Then to your left—westwards, then move it to the right—northwards again—to close the circle. Next, bring your bell (still ringing) upwards above the middle of your focal point (as above) and then move it down below the focal point or as low as you can go (as below) before bringing it back to the centre of the space and stop.

Next, put your cleansing tools to one side and begin the very personal and powerful act of populating your focal point with all your representations. Though some belief systems and schools of thought have guidelines for where things ought to go, I find this can be very constricting and not very personal. I would prefer that you place your items exactly where they are both safe and look and feel right to you—after all, it is your sacred space, your little gateway to creation, inspiration, and support. All I would advise (which is practical, rather than having any particular spiritual or energetic significance) is to give everything a good dust or clean before placing it down. Again, as with all things of this nature, you can invest as much or as little of yourself in this process as you choose; you may want to talk with each item as you place it down. Remember, this is somewhere where you will come, in good times and bad, to reflect on or to draw upon. So, the more time you take now to set it up with reverence and consideration, the better.

Once created, with everything in place, you may want to spend some time with your focal point straight away. Or leave it a day or two and then "visit" it. When you do, what you have created is a personal, accessible source of inspiration, creation, emotional sustenance, and support. You have created a space that invites in and "holds" energies of the elements, the directions, your spiritual heritage, and what you hold dear now. It is, in effect, a tiny, living temple to you! Come to this place whenever you feel a need to connect to all that it represents; you may have questions, concerns, want to share ideas, or shed a tear... there is nothing that you cannot bring before this space.

Visiting your Focal Point

There are no hard and fast rules that apply to how you use or how often you visit your focal point. You will know when it feels proper or necessary. I consider mine someone I can confide in and listen to, much like being with a wise elder or friend, especially when I look upon my representations of loved ones. I am also often drawn to lighting the candle I have for "fire" to inspire me or address my negative thoughts. I have a bowl of water (that gets topped up rather too infrequently) as my representation of water that I may dip a finger into or gaze upon when it comes to matters of the heart.

The main point is that during the time I spend here, I am stilling my mind and thinking, focusing only on one or two matters and, in so doing, putting my creative power to better use than worry or doubt. It is this simple connection to an energy both of you and of something greater than yourself. This is the same reason that more centralised "focal points" like temples, churches, and mosques were created.

Your Questions Answered

Right now, you may have some questions, or at the very least, some curiosities. There may be situations or events in your life that stir strong emotions: fear, uncertainty, or anxiety. These emotions may be driving you to either act too quickly and rashly, or paralyzing you into complete inaction or denial. Neither place feels comfortable or sustainable, so we all should aim to step back safely to then take life head-on. For example, the power to create may drive you to take control over what you do for a living. You could be looking for a career change or be frustrated by what you see as injustices working for others rather than getting your due rewards by working for yourself. So, before you suddenly hand in your notice or tell your boss what you think, retreat to your focal point and seek guidance.

The element of water, which connects directly with our emotional state, should be addressed, either by holding your representation of water in your hands or by dipping a finger into your bowl of water and wetting the middle of your forehead and each temple. What you need water and the ancestors to help you with at this point is to "calm the waters" and enable you to see more clearly the potential outcomes of the decisions you are about to undertake. To help you with this, you can close your eyes and ask—*please help me see the options I have and the various outcomes these options will lead to.* Or, suppose you like mantras or invocations. In that case, you can repeat the following three times: *to still my agitation and quell my troubled mind, so I may see more clearly the answers I fail to find, I call upon this blessed water to help decisions flow, and ask events unfold with ease revealing my time to go.*

Now it is just a case of remaining still; close your eyes, and allow all the subsequent thoughts to pop in and out of your head, like an idea smorgasbord. There is no rush. Take your time, see what feels right, what ideas and outcomes are the most comfortable for you. Over the next few days or so, you can review these thoughts, including the consequences, share these ideas with those you trust, and see what they think. And then, when it feels right, make your choices and carry them out. You will now be calmer in doing this after consideration, with a better understanding of what comes next and how to deal with it. Your emotions now become the passenger in your decision-making about your employment, rather than potentially recklessly driving the whole thing into a brick wall.

Creating and visiting your focal point invites you to take a moment to renew your bond with your inner self and spirit. When you create such a place, it encourages stillness, and it will help you reflect, explore, and bring some order to your thoughts and ideas—and bring you to a point where all things are equal. You are of a better mind from this place of equilibrium to see things from a more neutral position. You will be open to all the possibilities and outcomes of your decision making—the potentials and the pitfalls. With the principle of equality in mind, it is time to tap into our next goddess's teachings, a goddess who, it is written, defied inequality, the first woman on earth, according to the early monastic belief—Lilith.

Lilith's Legacy of Equality

Equality should always be a consideration in the life we create for ourselves. By that, I ask you to look at everything you bring into being, be it thought, word, or deed, and consider how this will impact those it touches, including yourself. A classic example of this, according to Hebrew mythology, the Babylonian Talmud, the Zohar, and the Alphabet of Ben Sira, is found in God's first mortal creations—not Adam and Eve, as one might expect, but Adam and Lilith. Lilith was created at the same time as Adam, not of Adam, and was said to dwell with him in Eden as his equal. But rather than ruling together, Adam was made the king of Eden. Lilith was confident and wise and soon wearied of Adam, who was less so. When Adam wanted to sleep with her, she questioned why she should be the one to submit and lie under him. The continued imbalance sees Lilith unashamedly quitting Paradise rather than being submissive.

Disharmony and an imbalance between the sexes is perhaps the most apparent outward example of our inner imbalance, the battle between change and resistance to it, and the emotional response this creates. And suppose you are constantly spending your energy fluctuating up and down or swinging side to side. In that case, your emotions are seldom balanced, but bouncing back and forth between unsustainable "highs" and suffocating "lows." But this does not need to be the case. When Lilith appears to you, it is a sign that either what you have created or undertaken, or what you are about to create, needs to be thought through or needs a firmer footing. Releasing your power to bring something forth is most successful when you have done your homework, and all things are relatively equal.

Lilith is most drawn to you when you are in a quandary or feel hard done by. She may speak, her voice soft but manner stern; she will be direct. Focus on what is said, because her physical presence can be intoxicating and distracting. This goddess is a sight to behold, especially if her snake is with her. There is no need to fear; she just wants to get the facts across to you and encourage you to do what is right, however uncomfortable. To tap into Lilith's energy, say, *Alluring serpents slip and slide, secrets whispered deep inside. All are equal, but don't back down; master this, you'll wear the crown. By the power of Lilith inside me, protection in place. Blessed Be.*

◎ CREATING AND USING A STONE SPIRAL

One of the oldest practices to bring us back into balance and harmony and to restore a sense of equality is to connect directly to the heart of our earth's energetic source by walking upon it in a very deliberate and mindful manner. Variations of this compelling practice include labyrinth work, and it can also occur in wheel work of various cultures. This is a way of connecting to your masculine and feminine energies via a universal spiral symbol. We see it in the natural world, in plants like the ancient ferns unfurling, or in the powerful vortices of weather systems and even within our DNA helix. In its emptiness, the quiet centre of the spiral was the source of all possibilities and the primal origin of all forms. From the centre, space reaches out into infinity, and it is this very centre that gives the impulse of motion to the spiral and all life.

YOU WILL NEED:

* A circular clearing or open space outside, approximately six meters in diameter

* Seventeen large stones, plus as many smaller stones or pebbles as necessary to define the lines of the spiral

Read through the guidelines a few times first to familiarise yourself with what you need to do once you have created the spiral; you want this to be as intuitive a process as possible.

Take time to find the suitable space; it may be more secluded, like a clearing in a wood, or as open as a beach at low tide; it might be in a field or even your garden. The most important thing is that it feels appropriate for you when you are walking in this space. It helps to cast your eye on the weather beforehand, too; this is not such an enjoyable exercise in driving rain or gale force winds! Be sure also to "ask permission" of this space—a simple task, just a matter of closing your eyes and asking for the time and energy allowed to hold this space as your own for the duration of this undertaking.

Next, collect the larger stones to lay out the form. Do this with "good intentions," i.e., as you select them, retain in your mind a vision of their use. Get a sense of each stone as you hold it, and ensure it serves its purpose willingly. Take only the stones you need and give thanks for their provision. Now pick the smaller pebbles to delineate the spiral (sand can be a practical alternative if you don't want this labyrinth as a permanent fixture). And now construct the shape by first marking the centre and the four cardinal directions (north, south, east, west) on the spiral's outermost line. As you move inward, do the same for the second, third, and fourth round of the spiral. Ideally, leave about two feet between the stones. (See Figures 1 and 2 below.)

Figure 1: Stone Circle Step 1

Figure 2: Stone Circle Step 2

After you have carefully laid out all the larger stones, connect them with smaller stones or pebbles, starting from the centre until you reach the entrance, which should ideally (but not necessarily) point north (see Fig. 3).

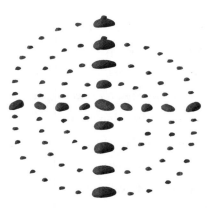

Figure 3: Stone Circle Step 3

At the entrance and exit, place two smaller stones on the large directional stones to serve as a gate marker. If you decide that this spiral is to serve as a more permanent fixture, you may also want to consider placing a large stone or piece of wood at the opening when not in use because this opening acts as an energetic gateway. Like this, the layout of a spiral creates an energy vortex that extends downwards into, and receives energy from, the earth, establishing a direct connection to all the creative power that comes from beneath your very feet. And with every conscious step you are about to take, the link is strengthened, and the energies increase. Now it's time to "awaken" the spiral. If the terrain and temperature allow, remove your shoes (socks too if you wish). Standing at the entrance, voice your intention by saying, *Harmonious energies of the earth, I return to you now. With each step, allow my being to be once again rebalanced, fill me with what I lack, and allow me to release what no longer serves, and in so doing, infuse me with the resolve to manifest my ideas with consideration for all those they may impact upon.* Now, with due care and attention, breathing in through the nose and out through the mouth, take the first steps into the spiral. Note how the ground feels beneath your feet; is it warm or cold, soft or hard? Imagine you are walking on a giant living being, so tread assuredly but gently, rolling your foot from heel to the ball of your toes as you proceed.

With one step, breathe in through the nose, and with the following step, release the breath through the mouth. With each step and in-breath, you are drawing energy up from the earth through your feet, legs, torso, and into your head. Let this energy gradually fill you and water the seeds of new ideas, long-forgotten plans, and hidden talents. With each step on the out-breath, you are releasing doubt, worry, and shame that have kept you stagnating, unable to let go and move on. Be mindful of every step; you are walking upon millennia of life forms, ancestors, plants, animals, and the life-giving force of Mother Earth; feel it all being absorbed through you, filling your heart with vigour. You may feel resistance to walk further at specific points or have the urge to turn and walk out or even run to the centre. Hold steady, take a few breaths, and then continue at an even pace. Walk purposefully, steadily, breathing in through the nose and out through the mouth until you reach the centre.

At this point, the energy is most amplified. Standing with feet parallel and eyes closed, take five deep breaths, being aware now of the sounds around you as you do—bird song, rustling, waves lapping, breeze blowing, whatever it may be—and allow your mind to explore any thoughts and visions as they arise. When you are ready, open your eyes, acknowledge the energy you have connected with, gently exit the centre, and re-walk the spiral breathing normally. When you have reached the entrance, thank Mother Nature for holding you in her space as you step out. If you chose to keep the spiral in place for a while, then "close" or "seal" the entrance by placing a branch or stone across it. Otherwise, you will need to gather everything and return it to where it came from, leaving the site as you found it.

The Baby and the Bathwater

This may be the first time you have journeyed to emotional self-mastery with the goddesses by your side. And if you are anything like me, there will be a temptation to wipe the slate clean and start from scratch. In other words, immediately make a list of what is and is not working in life right now, who you like or dislike, or even change jobs or move house "before" you begin this work. But that is the very opposite of what you should do. You can cope with all these things as they are. The lessons learned from Eingana and Lilith will help to bring you into balance and connect you with the right resources to face life and manage your emotions, as things stand right now. Even in times of turmoil or chaos, there is much to learn, much to be gained, and much to strengthen you for all that is yet to come in life.

It is about identifying, acknowledging, and balancing your inner needs and outer experiences. What is most fundamentally important and will save a lot of stress and complications down the line is to encourage and allow creativity to flow from you when you are stable and in balance, when you have that comforting feeling of a sense of inner assurance and calm. Don't fall into the trap of throwing the baby out with the bathwater. All the things you have experienced in life, all the people you have connected with, all you have done has brought you to this point. Honour that journey first, the things you have created thus far, and appreciate the lessons of your highs and lows equally.

The Power to Create, Resolution Tips

This may be the first "goddess" self-help book that you read, or you may be an avid follower of energy work or earth-centred practices. But whatever has drawn you to this book, it's essential to acknowledge that at the heart of your experience of this life is your emotional response, driven by the tremendous creative force coursing through your very being. So the sooner you can find a balanced place from which to draw on this force, the better, so remember:

> The urge to "create" to exist in some form is what motivates us, and it is at the heart of everything. You are a result of this energy, which can be channelled in many ways, including some techniques that can impact negatively, so the key is to master it in yourself and your daily life.

> Self-mastery begins with acknowledging and accepting that you will have times when things fail, go wrong, or break apart. It is precisely in these moments that the ability to return our anxious state and heightened negative emotions to a place of equilibrium is paramount.

The goddess Eingana represents the primal state of creation inherent in us all. Without any hidden agenda beyond the drive to bring forth life, she represents the purest form of our creative urge.

Remember that you have a connection to all you create; be prepared to take responsibility for your words and deeds.

Consider creating a "focal point" as a place of special dedication to pool the resources of creation, via the elements, the ancestors, and what matters to you, and it can provide clarity and guidance when needed, or hold a space for you, for whatever you need.

Equality, both internal and external, between individuals, groups of people, entire societies, and on a global scale is what we all strive for, even if only fleetingly, and provides the best platform to grow, create, and evolve. Though this may be a state impossible to sustain for long, it is a state you can frequently attain as a means to establish and maintain greater wellbeing in our lives.

The biblical story of "Lilith" demonstrates the chaos and frustration that disharmony and inequality create. It is a blunt example that even a force such as "God" can make mistakes when creating, when bringing forth ideas and desires without considering the consequences fully, or perhaps it is intentional to teach a lesson. That is a matter of your belief.

Creating and walking a stone spiral as a physical exercise requires consideration, planning, and determination. As a mental/emotional, even spiritual, exercise, it can be challenging, liberating, and ultimately a way to readdress the balance and restore internal harmony.

Don't throw the baby out with the bathwater; the foundations for change and getting emotional control are built on and strengthened by all that you have experienced, not just the good bits.

CHAPTER 2
The Relationship Ripple

We seldom create in isolation. What we desire or need to bring forth may require help, be it physical, emotional, or financial. Or our actions may affect others. My experiences and observations lead me to believe that relationships are predominantly founded on our emotional connection to another human being. During this process, we form and are connected by an energetic bond. From family, partners, and very close friends through to schoolmates, neighbours, and colleagues in the workplace, the quality of these relationships determines individual wellbeing. Getting relationships "right" can be a life-long undertaking. I have come to the conclusion that there exists what I like to call a "holy trinity" of relationships. And I see this trinity as the most significant for adults and especially women, consisting of the relationship with their life partner, the relationship with their offspring, and the relationship

35

with themselves. Some people will be juggling all three; for others, right now, it may only be two ... but for everyone, there is no getting away from the relationship with yourself. And when it comes to goddess energy within you, understanding, managing, and evolving who you are is perhaps the toughest of all your relationships. It can also be the most rewarding.

Gifts of the Goddesses

You are the most intriguing, complex, and influential person you will encounter in your life. Not because of all the things you already know about yourself, like what food you enjoy, what colours you like, what music you listen to, the films you want to watch, whether you stay up late or rise early ... that is all pretty rudimentary stuff. It is about the things you don't know. For example, you may have been brought up within a monastic faith, so much of the life experience as you know it will be shaped by that belief, especially your thoughts about those who do not share the same ideals. If what you believe resonates with you and you have a sense of calm and fulfilment, your faith could serve you well. It is also more likely that you will form relationships with those who either share the same faith or who at least are not in direct opposition to it. However, much like all our preconceptions, what we think and believe will be challenged at some point. And it is then that our emotional resilience comes under fire.

The lessons of the goddesses in this chapter are influenced by the energies of the hemispheres. From the north is Pandora, the tremendously gifted deity of Greek origin; from the south, Hine-nui-te-pō (Hine) of Pacific Island pantheon. Both their myths are tempestuous and reflect what can happen when we swing too far in one direction, when curiosity overtakes caution in Pandora's case or when broken trust leads to separation in Hine's example. So it is vital to have the tools to undertake these lessons from a neutral standpoint. You can again employ meditation at this point. It will allow you to mentally strip away the clutter to make sense of your thoughts and concerns. Like all things, it takes practice, but once learnt, it is never forgotten.

◎ Living Flame Meditation

This meditation is fundamentally about giving your mind space and time to breathe. Initially, this may just be for a few seconds, then a couple of minutes, and eventually, ideally, you will be able to set aside ten to twenty minutes at a time.

You will need:

* A quiet space where you can sit either on the floor or at a table where you will be undisturbed for ten to twenty minutes

* A candle (white or natural) in a candle holder of your choice and something to light it with

Sit down on the floor or at a table. Check that you are comfortable, and place the candle in front of you. Make sure you have a clear view of the top of the candle. Light the candle and reposition it if need be, to ensure you can focus clearly on the flame. While breathing normally, look at the flame for thirty seconds to a minute, avoiding anything else around it, looking only at the flame, taking in its shape and movement. Notice the different intensities of light and shade and how the vision around the flame softens till all you have in your view is the flame; then, after at least thirty seconds, gently close your eyes. The flame will have left an imprint, and that is now what needs your attention. This imprint usually appears as a bright swirling shape in a dark void. The flame may appear in several colours; pink, white, black, blue; what is vital is that you keep that flame in your mind's eye for as long as possible. Just focus on this shape, allowing any thoughts that come to mind to pass simply. Pay no attention to them, concentrating only on the form before your inner eyes, its colour and movement. As soon as the form fades from your mind's eye or you find your mind wandering to other things, open your eyes and focus on the candle flame before you.

Again, while breathing normally, just look at the flame. This time you probably won't need as long, say for just twenty to thirty seconds; avoid anything else around it, look only at the flame, taking in its shape and movement as before. Notice once more the different intensities of light and shade, and again how the vision around the flame softens until all you have in your view is the flame, then close your eyes again. The flame's imprint will return and, as before, keep that flame in your mind's eye for as long as possible. And, as last time, focus on this shape, allowing any thoughts that come to mind to pass simply. This being the second time you have the flame in your mind's eye, you may find it is easier to retain the image for just a little bit longer. Once it fades away again, simply open your eyes and blow out the candle in front of you. This living flame meditation is not about resolving the things that challenge you but instead preparing you to better cope with them. Remember, this meditation practice sets out to give you a clean slate to process your thoughts—a little mental spring cleaning, if you like. Like all things unknown to us, it takes time to get the hang of, no pressure but persevere; it will be worth it.

As vessels of universal creative energy, there is a wealth of clarity, ideas, and wisdom within us, but seldom do we allow the space and time for it to manifest. Both of these meditations develop the knack of watching passively, and once we know how to watch passively, we can be so much more in control of the activities in our daily lives. This is important because knowing and accepting what we are capable of and having the self-discipline and control to manage our emotions and how our body reacts prevents us from falling victim to chaos. This idea of chaos unleashed in our minds and played out in our physical body through a lack of self-mastery is graphically illustrated by our next dark goddess encounter, the much-maligned Pandora.

We Are All Gifted

We are all pretty special to have made it this far in life; to have survived long enough to be reading this book is a feat in itself when considering all the things that might have happened to us before this point. Just by being born, you have defeated great odds already! But our talents, the way we are, and what we can do are quite something else again and if we are taught to recognise and make the most of them in our lives, quite extraordinary experiences await. Abilities can vary enormously, from the very physical, like strength, agility, or flexibility, to the psychological, like intelligence, wit, empathy, and compassion. You may also have other talents that you would consider just a part of who you are. This could be a strong connection to animals, or an ability to "read" people and the natural world well; perhaps you sense things more than most or can connect with the metaphysical realm. Many people will say metaphysical/sensory abilities are "gifts."

When we speak of "gifted" individuals, it can often be a double-edged sword. The Greek goddess Pandora's name is also said to mean "all gifted," and so the scene is set that sometimes we must pay particular attention to what we are given and, more importantly, how and when we use it. This is important because, as we are discovering, what we create, what we think and do, will impact others. Remember, when we use our powers to create, we are seldom alone. At first glance, the story of Pandora can be seen as somewhat misogynistic, a woman created only to enchant a Titan and, in turn, unleash evil on earth. Convenient but far too simplistic and inaccurate when we look more closely at this goddess Pandora and see her as the teacher rather than the temptress.

The story of Pandora dates back to the early centuries of humanity, just after the Great War between the Titans and the Olympians. At a gathering of the ancient Greek gods and the Titans, the Titan Prometheus tricked the god Zeus into accepting a sacrificial offering that was nothing but bones covered in fat rather than prime cuts of meat. Humiliated and infuriated, Zeus set out to get even with Prometheus. He ordered Hephaestus, his master craftsman, to create a woman of such incredible beauty that she would be irresistible to men and gods alike, using Aphrodite, the goddess of love, to pose as inspiration.

Hephaestus crafted the body of earth and water; then, the Four Winds breathed life into her. Aphrodite bestowed her with grace. The messenger god, Hermes, gave her cunning of mind and mouth; Athena, goddess of wisdom and handicraft, gave her dexterity and dressed her. From Poseidon, the god of the sea, she was given a pearl necklace to guard against drowning. Apollo, the god of many talents, including music, taught her to sing and play the lyre. Zeus bestowed upon her a mischievous and idle nature, and finally, the great goddess Hera gave her curiosity. And so, according to this tale, Pandora is created, and with a highly decorated vase (the box mutation came much later), she descended to Earth. Now that is the most commonly-told version of the tale. Among many scholars, Pandora is seen and venerated as another goddess who resided along with the other great deities like Athena and Hera; however, much later and perhaps more to prove a point, we get the following story added on.

Learning to Box Clever

So we continue with the tale of Pandora and her now re-envisaged "box" of tricks. It was love at first sight for Epimetheus, Prometheus' brother, when he saw Pandora, and without a second thought, he proposed to her. At the wedding, Hermes revealed to Epimetheus that Pandora was a peace offering from Zeus to demonstrate no ill feelings between the gods and Prometheus. Epimetheus believed it all despite Prometheus' advice not to accept anything from Zeus. Time passed, and all seemed well, but Pandora's curiosity was getting the better of her—what was in the box? It began to consume her every waking thought.

Then one day, and despite vowing never to open the box but unable to control her curiosity any longer, she waited till she was alone. Then carefully taking the golden key that had hung temptingly around her neck, she unlocked and lifted the lid... It is said that in that very instant, an awful smell and spine-chilling sound were released from the box to fill the air all around her. So shocked and horrified was Pandora that she closed the lid, but it was too late, and the damage was already done. Pandora had inadvertently unleashed all that was unholy and malevolent that Zeus had locked in the box: sickness, death, strife, jealousy, hatred, famine... Pandora now realised she was part of a terrible act of revenge. The weight of the world bore down on her. However, not all was lost. Along with those terrible afflictions, Pandora had also revealed hope, the one good thing trapped inside the box. So it was said that hope would reside with humanity forever, to give succour in its darkest hours and just when all felt lost. And so the modern phrase "Pandora's box" was born to refer to an action that provokes many evils, yet hope remains; things can be changed.

So who really is Pandora to us? She is a goddess with incredible qualities and immense powers of manifestation and change. She is the box of tricks, within which await all manner of outcomes that can be released according to our actions. For every talent or gift we possess, there will be a counter; for every skill we choose to employ, there will be knock-on effects. You have the opportunities in life to discover your gifts and use them wisely, and just as importantly, manage the consequences. This is what is meant by "boxing clever." The first step is to discover what is within you, what you are capable of. Meeting Pandora is an excellent place to start.

You will sense Pandora's presence through the realisation of your talents. She is most present in your reflection, in your inner self taking shape, manifesting outwardly in your life. One of the best ways to discover all you are and what you have to offer to the world is through what is more commonly known as "mirror work," a term phrased by author and self-help advocate Louise Hay, who wrote that mirror work "reflects back to you the feelings you have about yourself. It makes you immediately aware of where you are resisting and where you are open and flowing. It clearly shows you what thoughts you will need to change if you want to have a joyous, fulfilling life."[1] Practical introspection as a means of gaining self-realisation is not new.

Mirror Work as It Once Was

An ancient practice encompasses the many uses of reflective surfaces to gain insight, either into the past or the future, as a form of divination. "Scrying" is the umbrella term given to this practice, often associated with old magick, witchcraft, and shamanism, but it is also referred to in the monastic religious texts. Prior to mirrors being available, people used highly polished, often dark materials like black obsidian or quartz crystals and, most common, bodies of still water. And long before visions manifested and fortunes could be told, the first thing a practitioner would see would be themselves. This ability to see yourself, initially as others do, but then to delve deeper into yourself, takes courage, but it is worth it.

As a youth, I enjoyed public speaking and debating. The idea that my words could move other people, even change their opinions, was so rewarding. I would spend hours in front of the bathroom mirror at home, practising my speeches, working on my facial expressions, body language, and tone. And through the mirror, I would sense what I hoped my audience would too: my confidence, sincerity, and belief that they could be empowered by what I said. In the early days, I just used the mirror to perfect the performance, but as time passed, I understood the mirror was showing me far

---

1   Louise Hay, "What Is Mirror Work?" https://www.louisehay.com/what-is-mirror-work/.

more and feeding my senses. If I was giving a speech, I could see the hall full of people smiling and nodding, feeling them take the journey with me. The mirror was no longer just acting as a reflection but as a tool for honing my talents and manifesting outcomes. That is only one example of self-realisation leading to self-actualisation. You can practise this too; just remember it takes a while to work beyond the reflection, but perseverance will deliver results.

◎ SELF–SCRYING EXERCISE

Self-scrying is not about predicting the future, seeing or divining it for others; it is purely to gain knowledge and understanding of who you are, how you project that to the outside world, and what you can do to better hone your talents. Remember also that this tool is only and specifically for you to use.

YOU WILL NEED:

* A mirror; ideally this will be made of naturally dark stone or crystal that, when highly polished, produces a reflective surface. The most accessible would be a black obsidian mirror. Alcohol-based natural detergent and a soft cloth to clean the reflective surface, and either cotton, linen, hemp, or silk bag to store the scrying tool when not in use

* A stand or surface on which to rest the scrying tool; this makes it easier for you to look at and work with

* A small handheld bell for clearing the space
  before scrying

Begin by creating and preparing your sacred space, ringing a bell in the four directions, and then call upon your guides, ancestors, or Source to assist you. Next, clearly state your intent for greater self-awareness and mastery. Now place the mirror on a table or on the floor, whichever is most comfortable for you. Once you're ready, close your eyes and begin to relax; feel every part of your body becoming relieved of all tension. Breathe in for a count of four, hold for four, and then release for four, and repeat as you relax further. Continue for a few more moments. Reaffirm your purpose again, and then open your eyes and focus on the mirror. Stay relaxed; it is okay to blink when necessary. Just allow your gaze to look upon the reflective surface; you will see a vague image of yourself. Smile and acknowledge your own being. Now sitting before your mirror, begin to imagine objects representing key aspects of yourself, like your favourite colour, a character trait, a gift, a favourite place. For example, if that colour was blue, imagine a blue balloon floating on the surface of the mirror. Then a character trait could be your ability to comfort people with your words, and for this, you might imagine an old large much-loved book of fairytales opening itself on the surface of the scrying mirror. Your gift might be an affinity to commune with nature, and so you might imagine a beautiful rose opening up on the surface of the mirror. And finally, your favourite place might be a beach from childhood, and for this, it is a delicate shell that you see on the surface of the mirror. One after another, use objects to represent all different parts of you and see them appearing in the mirror before they fade into the next one.

Continue to breathe deeply and steadily, close your eyes, and take three deliberate breaths in and out to the count of four, just as you did at the beginning of the exercise. And when you are ready, open your eyes. And that is all you have to do for your first time. Initially, by undertaking this exercise for just fifteen to twenty minutes a day, you will be able to exercise your creative mind into manifesting what is within you. This is such a useful tool as, with practice, you will be able to recall objects that will instantly connect you to your gifts and individual traits at will. Undertaken diligently, this self-scrying exercise can also be applied to your emotional triggers, so if you are easily angered, you might imagine seeing a red flag waving on the surface of the scrying mirror. Subsequently, if something triggers anger in your relationships, rather than "exploding," you conjure up the red flag. As soon as you see this, it too will fade with the anger, which is a great way to manage overwhelming or destructive emotions.

Tips for Charging Your Mirror

Some people find it helpful to "charge" their mirror with "light." Though this is always recommended when using a scrying mirror for divination, it can also be helpful (though not necessary) when using it for self-scrying. You can do this in two ways, so go with whatever feels most appropriate for you or the occasion. Do it before using the mirror to aid clarity and positivity, and to minimise distractions. The first method is by working with channelled light, harvested through simple meditation. This is ideal just before using your mirror. With your scrying mirror out of its bag in front of you on a table or the floor, close your eyes and take three deep breaths to the count of four: inhale for four counts, hold for four, and exhale for four. Feeling relaxed, imagine white light being channelled down from the top of your head, collecting in your torso until you become a vessel of pure white light. Remember to breathe fully, deeply, and rhythmically.

Next, move your arms, so the palms of your hands are facing each other in front of your chest and channel the light to the space between your palms, forming a ball of light energy. When you feel ready, project this ball of light onto the mirror's surface and visualise the light "soaking" into the mirror. Continue to repeat this process of forming a ball of light and projecting it into the mirror until the mirror "feels" full. Now state in your mind that the charge will remain as long as it is needed. Open your eyes, allowing any light within you to return to Source and begin to work with the mirror or place it back in its bag till required.

The second method takes place when there is sufficient moonlight in the night sky to shine down upon the mirror. On such a night, and in particular, a full moon, remove the mirror from its bag and, placing it on a tray, take it outside and place it in direct moonlight. Claim your intention to charge the scrying mirror with light for the purpose of self-scrying and leave it there overnight. Return to it at dawn and bring it back into the house, wipe the surface if necessary, and state in your mind that the charge will remain as long as it is needed, before placing it back in its bag till required.

Learning to manage your highs and lows and getting to know yourself, warts and all, is about understanding what you are really good at and where you can improve things or even avoid them. This is the solid ground from which all your relationships can flourish and give you the ability to know when to cultivate a relationship and when it is time to let a relationship go. This is particularly important when encountering the other two key potential relationship arenas in your life, the one with your closest kin and the one with your most significant others.

Our Real-Life Mirrors

The real-life mirrors come in two forms: those with whom we have the strongest biological connection, that of a parent, sibling, or child; and those who come into our lives to mirror back to us life lessons and rewards—our physical partners. I have found that both of these types of relationships trigger strong emotional reactions in love and life. Undoubtedly the most challenging of these is our own flesh and blood, for whom we feel the most tremendous sense of responsibility—our children, and this could also include adopted children. As mothers, we are mostly hardwired to protect and nurture our offspring, even to the detriment of our wellbeing and the consideration of others. It is a challenge, both life-affirming and heartbreaking, and one that I am still working through with my teenage children, especially my firstborn, my only son.

Much has been discussed when it comes to the maternal bond, from Sigmund Freud's oedipal complex to Donald Winnicott's belief that, during the first year of life, the mother and child constitute an indivisible psychic unit. Consider how we as mothers manage our emotional bond with our children, especially as they come into their own being with more complex demands and their own emotional triggers. And for those without children, this information and the alternate approaches can be used to manage the bond to your closest parent. It is worth noting that at the very core of this relationship dwells the goddess energy in its most potent form. To your child, you are the universe.

To create, nurture, and grow another life within your being is something both miraculous and instinctive. This experience ties you to all the creator goddesses and to the incredible energy that powers all life throughout the cosmos. The new life you bring forth shares half their genetic makeup with you, just as you are made of the stuff of your parents and the generations before. In this way, a primary "toon" or cord continues back to the heart of everything, creating another part of the vast web of life that extends across our world and beyond.

Closer to home, those so intricately connected to us also reflect both the traits we are proud of and the qualities we find less desirable, or even refuse to acknowledge. How many times have we noticed something in a child and said, "oh, that's just like your mum when she was little, so bossy" or "he takes after you … can't get a word in." We just laugh it off at that stage, but by the time they reach their teens, it's a whole different ball game. When "our" traits manifest in others and are used back at us, it is no longer amusing; for example, what we once considered "clever" about ourselves, we now see as "smart-mouthed" in our child. We feel the intense emotions for our children now take a different form as we go on the defensive.

When you are hurt or offended by those you love, consider how you feel. Putting ourselves in this state also has physical reactions like raised blood pressure, increased heart rate, and muscle tension in the face, all observations also made by Charlotte van Oyen Witvliet in her 2001 study on the application of "forgiveness."[2] Being able to apply forgiveness almost instantly when confronted by our child opens the floodgates to managing the brewing emotions. This is not making excuses for the child's actions but rather a way of avoiding resentment and verbal retaliation in the heat of the moment, and a breakdown of trust in the long run.

---

2   Charlotte van Oyen Witvliet, Thomas E. Ludwig, and Kelly L. Vander Laan, "Granting Forgiveness or Harboring Grudges: Implications for Emotion, Physiology, and Health," https://journals.sagepub.com/doi/10.1111/1467-9280.00320.

◎ Tipping the Bowl Visualisation

The following visualisation will help keep you in the right frame of mind. The more you practise it, the more confidence you will have when a situation arises and tempers flare. Just knowing that there is light at the end of the tunnel makes any confrontation less volatile and already puts you in a better frame of mind from the outset. Managing your emotional responses makes it easier to relate to your child and helps you address issues from a place of clarity that will help to reassure your child they are being heard and that you are both on the same side. Many indigenous people worldwide have a version of this practice, releasing acquired experiences and feelings that either no longer serve you or have become burdensome. The more adept you become at it, making it a part of your weekly or daily routine, the easier it will become and the greater the benefits will be.

You will need:

* A quiet space where you can sit undisturbed for five to ten minutes

* An empty vessel, like a cereal bowl, small basket, or large abalone shell

Having found your quiet space, with the vessel in hand, sit down on a chair, settee, or floor, and loosely hold your vessel right side up in your lap. Just relax and breathe normally through the nose. Now close your eyes. Become aware of the vessel in your hands, feel its weight in both hands, and imagine it as clean and empty. Notice how light it feels, almost as if it were about to levitate out of your hands. Next, with your mind's eye, stare into the vessel and see a brilliant ball of white light filling the bowl, radiating outwards. This is what your perfect "bowl of light" looks and feels like when all is well. Slowly open your eyes and put the vessel down on the floor or on a table. Stand up and shake out your arms and legs.

What you are about to do next will be the process of "tipping your bowl," because from this moment on, when you come to work with your bowl, you will not find it as it once was, full of light. So again, take your vessel, be seated comfortably, and place the bowl in your lap right side up. Now close your eyes and breathe normally through the nose. Recount your last few negative interactions with your child and focus on the various emotional responses. For each feeling of anger, hurt, frustration, and lack of control, see a small stone or pebble manifest itself and drop into your vessel. Feel your vessel become heavy under the weight of the stones and notice how the stones block out the light. Your vessel will feel uncomfortable to hold. It is no longer a brilliant bowl of light, directing energy to you from the Source of all life, but it has become a dull, cumbersome burden, starving you of energy as you cling on to the feelings of hurt, anger, and frustration. But no longer.

Visualise the stones tumbling out of the bowl as you now tip it upside down. And as the stones fall out from your bowl, watch them disappear into the floor, taking with them all the ill-feeling; all the hurt, the anger, the pain, the disappointment. Breathing normally all the while, turn the bowl right side up again in your hands and refill the vessel with the brilliant light of your goddess energy. As you do so, allow that feeling of "light" to ease its way into your being. Now open your eyes, put aside your vessel and go about your day. The key now is to become so familiar with this visualisation that whenever you feel overwhelmed, unbalanced, or weighed down due to your relationship encounters, you can do this and immediately and effectively release yourself of the emotional burden. And remember, even though this visualisation is tied in with your child, it can be used at any time, with anyone to whom you are close.

No one is perfect, and mistakes will be made, tensions will run high. The relationship that requires the most room for manoeuvre when mirroring our own traits comes from our "beloved" or significant other. You have far more control over this than you realise; after all, you chose this person. This relationship is also the most complicated when dealing with our emotions and channelling our creative energy. Often in a desire to make this relationship work, above all else, we may not see everything for what it is and may even choose to overlook warning signs. We can place our trust in a situation or a person all too quickly and too easily, and it is at these times that our next goddess, Hine, can make her presence felt.

In Our Emotions We Trust

The Great Goddess of the Underworld, Hine-nui-te-pō (Hine), now calls you from the Pacific Islands' hearts and minds. Gentle sounds of ocean waves and fern fronds' unfurling can be heard, along with bird song and a soft voice beckoning "*hāere mai*" (come here). Hine is a sight to behold, should you have the fortune to encounter her; skin tanned and tattooed, hair long, thick, dark, and wavy, falling down to her waist, a most shapely body, but powerfully built. Her symmetrical face is home to large brown eyes, a soft broad nose, and full lips, blackened by tattoo ink. She is the embodiment of the triple goddess, with all the elements of the maiden, mother, and crone rolled into one. But the subtle creases in her face, the stray grey hairs lying defiantly amongst the black waves down her back also tell of a life lived and born out of necessity rather than desire. This is her story. In the Land of the Long White Cloud (now known as Aotearoa or New Zealand), all the children of Mother Earth (Rangi) and Father Sky (Papa) were born male. Tāne, the god of forests and birds, was the first to look for a wife. Unable to birth a wife for him, Rangi showed Tāne how to mould a companion from the earth. Tāne then breathed life into the body of earth, and Hine-ahuone came to life. It was not long before a daughter was born. Hine-ata-uira (later to become our goddess Hine), known then as the maid-of-the-flashing-dawn. Tāne takes her as his wife also, and in time they too have children. All seemed well until one day, while Tāne was away, Hine-ata-uira found herself lost in thoughts of her ancestry. She soon discovered that Tane was not just her husband with whom she had borne children and trusted above all others, but also her father. Her trust shattered; she was so overcome with shame that she ran off in despair. Deep in the forest, with the vegetation thicker, light fading, she finds herself at the entrance to the Underworld.

When Tāne returns and is told that Hine has gone to the spirit world, he goes after her. Through the forest he runs, as the light fades around him, until he reaches the entrance to the Underworld. To his surprise, he is prevented from entering by Hine herself, in her new role as goddess of the Underworld. She tells Tāne to return home and raise their children and that she will remain here in the Underworld to gather them in when the time comes. So Tāne goes back to the upper world, while Hine stayed below. However, there is another twist in the tale. When mortal man, represented by Māui, attempted to cheat death by passing, headfirst, through Hine's body, the sight of a man trying to enter this deity headfirst through her legs was too ridiculous for the birds, whose laughter stirred Hine. She awoke to the horror of a man trying to enter her without her permission. In closing her legs swiftly, she crushed him and, with that, brought about the cycle of death and rebirth to all humanity.

The Scorned Goddess

Hine-nui-te-pō felt wronged twice over, something that can happen to us all when trust is betrayed, particularly by those we love. You may have an immediate need to exact revenge, to want the other person to experience the pain you feel, to have them hurt like you do or disappear off the face of the Earth altogether. We cannot exact revenge by crushing every person who does us wrong, however; we don't want to live forever in the dark, so to speak. One way out of this darkness is to acknowledge our pain and then to forgive. And yes, forgiveness is easier said than done, so I want you to think about "forgiveness" simply as another tool to untie you from the pain of the situation. Forgiveness as a tool is about helping you, more than the perpetrator, cut yourself free from the weight of the negative emotions that stir within.

To forgive what that person has done to you does not mean you are letting them off the hook. Neither does it mean you can just forget it ever happened, for if people simply went about forgetting the past deeds, they would be at risk of repeating them repeatedly. No, the goddess approach to coming to terms with what is done, what that action has caused, and how to resolve or manage it looks more practical. The goddess seeks to cut you free from the emotional bondage. In doing so, you will be able to transform your emotions and separate that which no longer serves from that which is still nurturing and sustaining you. In the great tapestry of life, patches do become threadbare, and as the master weaver, it is for you to mend these patches, remove old threads for new.

Master Weaver

You may already be familiar with the idea of "cord cutting," a process by which negative, fear-based energy attachments are removed from your life. It is believed that these attachments are formed when you have imbalanced relationships with other people, for example. When we continue to engage in these relationships, the cords increase in number and drain away our energy, feeding the toxic situation developing. In addition to learning to identify what has become a drain in your relationship, cord cutting is both a helpful and quick resolution of adverse situations. However, as we know, when we create, we seldom create in isolation; all that we do becomes part of our great tapestry of life; every thread we weave, good, bad, or indifferent, plays an integral part in creating our picture as well as holding the picture together. When it comes to goddess energy, we look to work with threads rather than "cords."

And just like cords, we can remove threads, but better still, unlike cords, we can rework threads within our tapestry whilst still maintaining the integrity of the picture we are creating. Going back to the stories of both Pandora and Hine, we see their challenges as their tapestries become discoloured or threadbare. This is a better explanation than them being choked by the negativity of toxic cords. Their emotional dilemmas, the hurt, shame, and guilt, are managed by mending the tapestry rather than cutting the ties. In both cases, rather than cutting themselves off from life, the goddesses worked into the tapestry a vision of rebirth. Both goddesses play a vital role in the ending of life, and both (Pandora through "hope" and Hine through her custodianship of the Underworld) are also responsible for rebirth, for facilitating another chance to live or opportunities to bear fruit. Their emotions are not left to dwell on negativity, and the perspective shifts to one of resolution. Like them, mastering your feelings when it comes to your most important relationships will give you peace and enable you to move forward from a place of self-care and self-respect.

When we mend the threads, other persons involved can feel the shift, too; their tapestry is also altered. It can be that the other person suddenly thinks of you out of the blue, especially when this relates to a past relationship. It might prompt them to get in touch, or if it relates to a situation within a current relationship, it might prompt that person to want to revisit what happened. That's okay; so long as you choose a way forward that does not cloud your picture, keep your threads just as they are. Some of us can even be tempted to undo that part of the tapestry allowing old emotions to resurface. This is often the case of the "mother/child" scenario; I would be very surprised if it were not something that happens repeatedly; such is the nature of the bond of mother and child. Just remember, you are most powerful when your tapestry is unsullied.

◎ MASTER WEAVER VISUALISATION

As a mother, as a child, as a loving partner, and as your best ally, you have far more effective ways to use your talents to uplift others and yourself without it draining you, becoming a burden, or clouding the tapestry you are creating. When you rework or remove and replace threads, you open yourself and those around you to experience greater fulfilment, health, and peace. You can manifest your hopes and dreams with greater clarity and direction. The following visualisation will help you to do just that.

YOU WILL NEED:

* A quiet space inside where you will be undisturbed
* A small handheld bell for clearing the space
* Something comfortable to lie down or sit on

Once you have found your "sacred space," the place where you can practise this meditation without being disturbed, you need to energetically "clear" the space. Do this by taking your bell and clearing the four directions (full details of this can be found in Chapter 1 as part of "Creating a Simple Focal Point"). When you are done, put your bell to one side and lie down or be seated facing east, the direction of creativity. Now close your eyes and take four deep breaths to the count of four. Inhale through the nose for a count of four, hold for a count of four, and slowly exhale through the mouth for a count of four.

Repeat this three more times. Continuing to breathe steadily (no need to count), I want you now to imagine a field of wild grasses stretching before you, clear blue skies above you, and to either side gently rolling hills, populated with tall, dark green trees. Take your time and allow this image to manifest before you; wild grasses below, blue skies above, and green hills on either side, the frame of your tapestry taking shape.

Once you have this picture in your mind's eye, you will start to see a great image form in the middle before you, a great tapestry, beginning with a plain canvas and quickly filling with threads of all colours and materials, cotton, silk, wool, hemp, whatever you see forming the picture that depicts your life at this time. Watch as the threads interweave, creating landscapes, shapes, buildings, faces, whatever you see as representative of you and your life at this time. It is awesome and beautiful, full of movement and life. All the while, you continue to breathe in and out steadily.

Now just think about something troubling or niggling you in a relationship. It might be an angry word, ill-will, lack of trust, feeling of resentment, and I want you to look at your tapestry and see where in the amazing picture it is blurry, or threadbare, or stained. This will be where your negative emotions have been woven in and need to be reworked. So keeping those feelings in mind, steadily examine the tapestry till you sense or see the problem.

Now home in on the patch; you can even reach out to touch it and notice how it feels; it might feel rough, or sticky, or even start to disintegrate. You need to mend this now with care and attention. So with your mind's eye, you look to your right and notice a basket containing a pair of silver scissors, a large silver darning needle, and a ball of silver thread. You bend down and reach for the scissors; they feel cool in your hand. Now look to the patch that needs attention and cut loose any threads that don't belong, allowing them to fall freely to the ground below, or be carried off in the breeze. Next, take the silver thread and cut a length; go with your gut; it will fit just right. Thread the darning needle and stitch it into the tapestry, replacing what was cut away. Remember this is a visualisation, don't get hung up on exact details, like the length of thread or whether you can sew or not—it is all about your intention and the shift of energy; it will all find its place.

Look closely at your patch for any threads that might just be a little worn or broken and need to be repaired rather than replaced. To make this type of repair, just cut another length of silver thread and weave in over the top of the weaker threads as support. Stand back and look at your handiwork. Notice how the new silver thread takes on just the right colours to perfectly match in and mend that part of the tapestry just as it should be. Put the needle, thread, and scissors back in the basket. Remember, you can come back to work on this tapestry at any time and as often as you want or need to. Allow the tapestry to fade out of focus as you continue to breathe steadily, and then allow yourself to gently return to your room and open your eyes.

Practising this visualisation will get you comfortable and familiar with working on your tapestry, which in turn will give you the confidence to know that, should you find yourself challenged by someone you love, you have a way of dealing with the emotions that arise from it. You may even find that this quells your responses and even changes how you feel when things are happening—you are managing your emotions at that moment, which will affect the other party. Remember, understanding your emotional responses, your goddess energy, is always a work in progress, but the more tools you have to do that, the more practised you are at applying them, the easier it all becomes, no matter how long it takes; the tapestry is a life's work, but together we will make it a joy to weave, not a burden.

Relationship Ripples, Resolution Tips

Relationships are complicated, especially when it involves those we love the most, those we bring into this world, and ourselves. And nothing in this life makes it easy all the time. We cannot control other people, and when we begin to create and manipulate our own lives, we inevitably bring others into our orbit. What we can learn and practise is to manage how we react to the challenges that relationships throw up. We can harness our creative energy and channel our emotions in such a way that they enhance a situation, so please consider:

> By simply being ourselves, by doing what we do and manifesting our lives, we impact others; we seldom create in isolation. Understanding how we affect others, and our emotional responses to these interactions, will help us to manage the key relationships in our lives better, starting with ourselves.

> Make meditation part of your self-care routine, whichever form you choose; it will give you the mind and heart space to face your emotions, understand them, and apply them wisely. Use meditation to become the foundation of your inner temple, a place where you can connect to the goddesses and, with their help, work through those feelings and relationships that no longer serve you.

> We all have talents; discovering and understanding your gifts and how you employ them should be encouraged. The rewards come as an appreciation and understanding of what you are capable of.

> The goddess Pandora's story of unleashing all ills without control is a reminder that we, too, can trigger troubles when we act without consideration.

But we are capable of much more than being led by curiosity, and we can always resolve a situation so long as we still draw breath.

Self-scrying helps us to identify our emotions and develop coping methods when destructive feelings are triggered. Rather than burying these emotions, we manage them, using our energy more wisely and understanding why we feel that way.

Our relationships act as emotionally charged mirrors, reflecting some fundamental home truths. Our blood relatives share some of our traits, for better or worse, triggering emotions, whilst our partners tap into the energies in us that they need, and so we do the same.

Consider "tipping your bowl" as a form of exorcising pent-up feelings. Tipping your bowl keeps your energy in the process of renewal, recharge, and reuse, which is why so many goddesses represent an element of death and rebirth.

Trusting our gut or following our feelings is a primal drive, with the heart often overriding the head. And that is the most reliable and intuitive way we navigate our path, constructing our relationships, and manifesting our lives.

Hine's story touches on the power of our feelings and the damage that can be done when we are devoid of coping mechanisms, made to feel lesser than, when the world is not what it seems, when we are made to feel we can no longer trust in those we hold dear.

Weaving our life tapestry is about recognising that what we manifest is an ongoing work of art that can be altered, reworked, and repaired. Working on your tapestry is an act of healing, love, self-care, and divine energetic creation.

Chapter 3
Tackling Temptation

When relationships are formed, we value and need direction. However, very few people thrive in an unbalanced relationship, at the behest of others, forgoing their needs to ensure someone else's needs are met. It is important to recognise that we face other powerful emotions in these circumstances, like the desire and natural tendency to tempt and persuade others. Religious foundations rely on "followers" to conform in order to survive, and children use persuasion as a bedrock to getting their needs met as an intuitive tool to thrive, for example. And for millennia, masculine energy has dominated; men are considered the natural leaders and have had the power, both in a physical and financial sense. Women or those carrying the feminine energy have been told to accept this and expect it.

But this is far from the truth when it comes to using the pure creative power within. As a woman, understanding, accepting, and then mastering your creative energy through your emotional repertoire opens up a world of possibilities in relationships in which the balance of power is transformed. But if you use your power for the sole purpose of domination in your relationships, then I have failed you. This is about restoring equality and balance in your life.

Goddesses of Temptation

Generally, to be "tempted" implies that you are considering something that may not be for the greater good, which yields only a short-term gain, and could ultimately cause issues or pain to yourself or others. It might be something as trivial as eating an extra slice of cake, buying yet another pair of shoes when you have plenty, or staying up all night to binge-watch a TV series. But the type of temptation that can really impact our lives plays on our deep-seated emotions and can lead to dire consequences, such as addiction, criminal behaviour, and infidelity. And as beings who are learning to harness their goddess energy will know, cheating is as much an issue for women as it is for men.

I invite you to learn from the tales of two intriguing goddesses—Deer Woman from indigenous North American mythology (exerting a passive influence of temptation) and Uzume from Japanese Shinto mythology (exerting a more active influence of persuasion)—to look at the challenges they present you with and the ways in which you can draw from them, rather than being drawn into their strong, emotional whirlwind. Both of these goddesses can put your head in a spin. They may even drive you to consider coercive measures where threats or physical violence can be employed to make another person behave in a certain way or do what you want them to do, even against their own will or better judgement.

◎ NATURAL GROUNDING EXERCISE

As we encounter the goddesses, it is vital that you are as grounded or rooted in balance and harmony as you can be. Equally, if you get caught up or employ this energy, you need to return to a place of balance quickly. It is fitting that we turn to Nature for this place of sustenance and sanctuary. The purpose of this exercise is to ensure that you feel grounded and centred, and to strengthen your experience of being present in your physical body and supported by the natural world. Each element of the exercise can be experienced for as long as you wish. This exercise encourages an improved flow of goddess energy, propagates a sense of peace, and reconnects heart and mind. So now I will share with you this natural grounding exercise to achieve these objectives.

YOU WILL NEED:

* Either a quiet space in nature, ideally with trees, where you will not be disturbed; or

* Make space in your garden and have a representation of wood that you will place a few feet in front of you

(this could be a picture of a tree, an actual piece of driftwood, or any statue of meaning to you that is made of wood)

* A mat to stand on, if that is preferable to standing barefoot on the ground

Once you have found the best place to do this, remove your shoes and socks, so you can directly connect with the earth. At this point, if you prefer to stand barefoot on your mat outside, that's fine. If your outdoor space has no grass, that's fine too, as the energy will be strong enough to come up through decking, slabs, etc. Now, place your feet firmly on the ground, about shoulder-width apart. Focus on the sensations coming from your feet, starting with the sole. Does it feel that it is making firm contact with the ground, or perhaps the contact feels lighter, more elevated? There is no need to readjust at this point; we are just paying attention to the feeling right now and there is no right or wrong.

Next, move your attention to the balls of your feet and toes. Are they making a good connection? Do they feel warm, tingly, or as if they are spreading wider? Again, this is just an observation, no need to force anything. By merely placing focus on your feet, you will have released energy from your body to them and triggered a response from the earth beneath to do the same. Looking ahead now and allowing your arms to rest by your sides, close your eyes and take in three deep breaths. With your mind's eye, scan your body slowly for areas of stress. Starting with the head, look for any tension in the face or neck; if you see or feel it there, acknowledge it and then let it go. If it requires turning your head a little to release, then do so. As you move down through your body, you may want to drop the shoulders a little, or gently shake out your arms and legs, or wiggle your fingers and toes.

Now return to your breathing. If it is still slow and steady, tremendous, but perhaps it has become a little faster or more laboured. So again, take three deep breaths to slow things down; breathe in through the nose, pulling the breath into your stomach, feeling your rib cage and lungs expand, and out through the mouth, pushing the air out of your lungs. Return your focus with your mind's eye back to your feet and gain a sense of their connection to the earth; with this connection, you are about to become the tree, nature's link between Mother Earth and Father Sky, a conduit for goddess energy.

Visualise now your feet and legs descending into the cool earth, and as they do, roots sprout from your feet and spread sideways and downward, literally rooting you to the spot. You feel the cool ground enveloping your lower limbs in a gentle embrace that holds you firmly. You feel the roots connecting you to all the energy and power of the earth. Next, take a deep breath in from your roots through to the soles of your feet and up through your legs. Feel the breath, the energy continuing to expand into the trunk of your body. And as it does so, notice the trunk of your body taking on the form and qualities of the trunk of the tree you are becoming; stable, steady, resilient, but full of life.

Let your tree expand through your shoulders and along your arms to the tips of your fingers. On the next in-breath, gently raise your arms shoulder height with palms turned upwards; sense how strong yet supple these upper limbs are. Pull your arms back ever so slightly and allow your chest to expand as you take in another breath and fill your lungs. On the out-breath, imagine the energy coursing along your outstretched arms and allowing your hands and fingers to burst into blossom. You are a tree of abundance because you are so well-rooted and nourished. Bask in this beauty for a few breaths, and then relax your arms again by your side. On the next in-breath, pull it up from your roots, through your trunk and branches allow it to expand into your throat and up into your head, relaxing your every thought.

With the next couple of breaths, feel the energy fill your head and expand out into the sky above. With each in-breath, notice this cleansing force fill your being. With each out-breath, release all of the tensions in your body and negative thoughts in your mind into the sky. Continue to draw up energy from the earth to the crown of your head and out into the universe. Notice any thoughts that may come into your mind and then release them with each out-breath. Acknowledge these distractions, then let them go and focus again on your deep-rooted feet and legs, your sturdy trunk, and your far-reaching canopy.

Continue to breathe steadily, pulling up the energy from below, feel it cleanse your body, your mind. And when you breathe out, release the tensions and negativity. Repeat this process until you are relaxed, re-energised, and free from stress and tension. When you are ready, gradually focus your awareness back on your feet's soles and legs, sensing how the earth feels. You are truly grounded and connected. Now slowly but surely, focus on the roots you have made and gently draw them into your being, thanking Mother Earth for her support as you do.

Next, feel yourself rise up out of the earth as your legs and feet return to their natural state. Bringing your attention to your torso allows the bark of your trunk to fall away as your body takes its natural form; your hands are now free of blossoms and your arms are by your side. And allow the last of Earth's energy to leave your crown skyward as your head gently falls forward, chin to chest, and thank Father Sky for his help. Slowly breathe more regularly again and, lifting your head, open your eyes.

The Greener Grass of Pastures New

Often temptations of the flesh have been linked to the natural world. It is expressed by sayings like "the grass is always greener on the other side of the fence," and made famous by the most renowned tale of temptation, taking place within the garden of

Eden and involving a snake, the Tree of Knowledge, and an apple as the weapons of mass temptation. What rings true about both these accounts is that, as people of creative drive fuelled by emotion, we seek the best possible environment to create, grow, and flourish, be it physically or emotionally. You will look for those with whom you can be happy, those who can protect or provide what you lack. And you will look for the best environment to be in.

When you find yourself comfortable with good people, you are very unlikely to entertain thoughts of looking elsewhere. It is generally when you are unhappy, perhaps bored, or feel out-of-kilter or even threatened that you are nudged to look beyond what you know. If you are grounded, you can often work through these feelings to better understand why you feel as you do and, most of the time, make the changes to improve things without having to flee. But if we are not grounded, or lack the coping mechanisms to deal with this urge of escapism, then we are ripe for the talons of temptation to reach out to us and pull us in, however subtly, or quietly tighten their grasp on us.

Many tales across all cultures aim to give us, as children, either moral guidance or a warning of those things we should avoid. Stories of dangerous woods filled with wicked witches or child-eating wolves. The perils of giving in to our curiosity. The importance of telling the truth, doing as we are told, especially by our parents. The threat to avoid strangers and strange places. Generally, all tales that ultimately perpetuate the idea that "good" (as the adults see it) will always overcome "evil." As time passes and we reach puberty, new tales warn of the temptations and dangers of giving into lust, especially when they take the form of beguiling females. These temptresses are often entwined with the even greater forces of nature, becoming a part of it so powerful that none can resist. We have the sirens of the sea, for example, and on land many various forms of the enchanting Deer Woman.

Deer Woman stories, including sightings, exist in many Native American tribes like the Sioux, the Omaha people, the Otoe tribe, and the Pawnee people, Cherokee and Muscogee Seminole, Choctaw, to name but a few. She appears most often as a beautiful young woman from head to torso, with the lower body of a deer. Primarily associated with fertility, Deer Woman has the ability to extend her powers from that of a mere enticing glance across a wild meadow to the ability to trample incautious people to death, especially disobedient children or promiscuous men. There are many female spirits worldwide with similar characteristics. In Chile, Fiura uses magic to trick lustful young foresters into sleeping with her. In Europe, great deities have become the child-stealing, mind-bending, monstrous avengers of all those who have been tempted into evil action. But Deer Woman energy in its purest sense is what we can tap into today. This energy is most often expressed through the subtlest temptations; when your inner voice says, "Go on, it's okay to sneak a bar of chocolate on your diet." Or when you think it's okay to tell a white lie about your friend's new haircut (even though you know it doesn't suit her), when you take a sick day off work to go to the beach instead … and so on.

◎ PERCEPTION PRACTICE

We all partake in small temptations and think little of them. When you are tempted in this way, which can quickly be justified by "no harm done," the energy and influence of Deer Woman only skim the surface; her doe-like brown eyes are merely giving you an enticing glance from across a grassy spring meadow. You just see the flowers holding their heads to the sunlight, the butterflies flitting in the breeze from grass to plant, just feet above the beautifully carpeted land. And all this feels fine; she smiles at you, you smile back, but all the while, you, like all of us, are building your resistance to the deeds of darker things and seldom see this coming.

The longer you allow yourself to repeatedly ignore the little temptations, the more comfortable you become with the subtle alterations to your emotions—in particular, the intensity of the experiences you have that trigger your "warning" and self-regulating emotions, such as guilt, satisfaction, resistance, or patience. What will help you at this stage is to learn from the lessons of Deer Woman's story. This will enable you to regulate how often you give in to the little temptations of life. And most importantly, to be able to perceive the difference between those temptations that are harmless once in a while and those temptations that are not.

YOU WILL NEED:

* A small notepad/notebook and pen/pencil
* Honesty, will, and discipline

You won't need anything else specifically, but you will need to be honest with yourself and continue to "practice" this method until it becomes second nature, to the point that you do it subconsciously, if and when you need to do it at all, anymore. Ensure that you have your notepad and pen with you, or somewhere you can easily access it, each day. First, it is all about familiarizing yourself with the process on a very conscious level. As you go about your first day of this practice, from the time you wake to when you go to bed, take note of each incident that tempts you. It doesn't matter at this stage whether you manage to resist or give in; it just matters that you keep a log of each event. Just like a list, leaving a little space between each event (to add notes later).

For example, a day might involve getting up a little late. So do you decide to shower tonight, and for breakfast, you decide to grab a piece of leftover pizza and eat on the way to work? You approach a set of traffic lights on amber, take the risk and go through them just as they turn red. At work, things run quite smoothly, and at lunch, you get yourself a healthy chicken salad and give yourself the time to enjoy it. Later in the day, a few people gossip about a colleague during a coffee break; you listen but choose not to say anything, despite knowing it is grossly exaggerated. In the evening, you pick up a takeaway on the way home, stay up watching TV, then remember you need to shower, and by the time you get to bed, you are so tired you decide against calling your friend abroad and fall asleep. What would be noted down as temptations during this day as part of the practice would be as follows:

* No shower
* Pizza for breakfast
* Run the lights
* Go along with gossip
* Takeaway
* Watch TV
* No call

Now you take each point and look at the pros and cons. This is something that you might believe you do already, as second nature, with little choices through the day that are almost instantly justified. The thing is, Deer Woman energy exerts her influence, tempting us to often make the "easiest" choice or path of least resistance or instant gratification. We look to quickly justify what draws us most rather than what might be the better choice. But like all things, we can alter this pattern by first becoming aware of it and then reprogramming how we think over time. It just takes practice. You start by writing things down until this new way of reasoning becomes the norm.

So, looking at the list, you would note the following temptations' justifications (be as honest and candid as you can):

No shower—*saves time now, can always shower later*
(oh but have a phone call to make tonight, think
about it later), most important can save time . . .

Pizza for breakfast—*saves a bit more time, but not*
very healthy or filling, make sure to eat properly
later, tastes okay cold too, and saves time . . .

Run the lights—*saves time, I won't get caught, no*
cameras, won't do it again . . .

Go along with gossip—*not the time to say any-*
thing, will say something later, sure she won't
hear about it . . .

Takeaway—*easier than cooking, I'm tired, I had a*
good lunch, it's okay, won't buy a takeaway again
this week . . .

Watch TV—*lovely to relax a bit; it makes me laugh,*
other stuff can wait . . .

No call—*needed the shower, will text friend, too late*
to call anyway . . .

Finally, look again at each point and ask three times if there is
a better alternative. Some things may stay the same, but a lot
can change for the better. Learn which temptations you can
give in to and manage, and which temptations you can resist.

No shower—*have I got time for a shower? Not really. Do I need a shower now? Am I clean enough? Yes, not grubby, don't smell. Have I got time for one later tonight? Yes. Okay, will shower later; save time now...*

Pizza for breakfast—*Time for a decent breakfast? Possibly. Pizza in the fridge, should I just take a slice? Saves more time. Have a proper lunch later.*

Run the lights—*Might get caught on camera? True. Might even cause an accident? True. Can I afford to get points on my licence? No, okay, don't run the lights.*

Go along with gossip—*Do I have to go along with what is being said? No. Can I put the record straight? Yes. Is this a better outcome than allowing gossip to spread? Yes, okay, say something to set the record straight...*

Takeaway—*Have I got time to cook? Yes. Have I got the energy? Not really. Won't eat takeaway again for a while. Okay, will pick something up.*

Watch TV—*Will I enjoy the programme? Yes. Should I be doing something else first? Yes, shower and phone call. Okay, will put the programme on hold...*

No call—*Is the call urgent? Yes. Do I still have time? Yes. Can I shower after? Yes, okay, call my friend.* ...

And so the practice takes shape, writing down the small temptations each day and then discerning which really can be changed. In so doing, you have the potential to change the patterns of a lifetime, improve self-discipline, and save time and energy—it takes its toll continually having to justify things that are not quite right! You will find making better choices more straightforward, and you will find the time to prepare and stick by these choices. The more you invest in this, the more it will pay off.

Temptations of the Flesh

The shadow side of Deer Woman myth deals not with the myriad of choices we make every day but with a choice that many face, maybe more often than once or twice in a lifetime, and that comes in the form of a deeper desire. The long-held belief that we can find greater happiness with other people, either a life better than the one we have with the person we are with, or that we can provide a better life for another person than the one they have with somebody else, is perhaps the greatest temptation we face. Seldom is the grass greener. It can happen that the "right" person comes along, yet you may not be in a position to be with that person. Sometimes, people are so drawn to each other that they will give up anything to be together regardless of the consequences.

But most of the time, if such a temptation comes out of the blue when you aren't searching, when things seem okay, it is an opportunity to improve yourself and your current relationship rather than risk what you have. There is a saying that goes along the lines of, "you can get your appetite anywhere, but always eat at home"; in other words, you can look at all the things that are on offer but use the appetite it builds in you to improve what you have at home. Temptations turn our heads only when there is something we want to turn away from. So in a similar way to asking yourself questions over the little things, you can also write down and apply the same process to this greater temptation. Here, however, you are dealing with potent emotions, like lust, longing, or flattery pulling you; and longing, confusion, or dissatisfaction pushing you the same way.

Sitting down and applying your daily discernment practice when these emotions are stirred takes both courage and discipline, but it can be done. And much can be learned. It is a case of applying the "head" before deciding whether or not to follow the heart—if it even is a matter of the heart and not a case of disillusion or disenchantment. Feelings of great disappointment can creep up on us in life, especially if the little things that cause us concern always go unchecked. If the person you are with begins to grate, those little habits that you thought at first were quirky now drive you mad.

But you say nothing and do nothing; you don't allow that person to change these things. Without your partner knowing why, you may begin to resent them, and the magic you once felt between you now seems to fade. You open the door to invite in the energy of our next goddess. Years of living with a child you instinctively want to protect start taking their toll as they grow up and begin to take things for granted. But again, if all the little things have been left to go unchecked if your concerns are not voiced, opportunities for change go wasted. And this can be applied to any relationship of great importance to you that pulls at your heartstrings.

What begins to open up before you, in your heart, is a hole. The feelings of emptiness, failure, and despondence are growing within. But to now step away from what you know is not the same as being tempted to eat a bar of chocolate, buy a new pair of shoes, or run a red light. You can still feel this is a different matter altogether; you need to be persuaded to validate the changes you want to make. The energy that it takes is most eloquently encapsulated in our next goddess, Uzume.

Powers of Persuasion

Ame-no-Uzume-no-Mikoto, to give her full name, is a most revered Japanese Shinto deity. She is the goddess of the dawn, the creator of the performing arts, and she alone saved the world from eternal darkness by persuading Amaterasu, the sun goddess, to rise again. Uzume's name can be translated in several ways, including "the Great Persuader" or the "Heavenly Alarming Female." Uzume is first and foremost the goddess of dawn, placing her in the service of Amaterasu, the goddess of the sun. Traditional stories describe Uzume as wearing loose or revealing clothing; she is open, easygoing, and dedicated to bringing joy to the world. She is also considered an "inari kami," or a goddess connected to kitsune, Japanese fox spirits known for their cunning and wiles.

The great deed Uzume performed is told as follows. Amaterasu, the sun goddess, had been so terribly shamed by her brother Susanoo that she retreated into a cave, vowing never to come out again. No sun goddess also meant no sun, and the world was plunged into darkness and devoid of all warmth. Nothing and no one could convince Amaterasu to come out of the cave. However, the talented and creative Uzume came up with an idea, and together with the other heavenly deities, she made a plan. Uzume started to dance, teasing and jesting for all in front of the cave, as if it were her stage. She took off various pieces of clothing until she was almost nude. Her audience found this so entertaining and funny that they began to roll about with laughter.

Meanwhile, inside the cave, Amaterasu could hear the laughter, and she grew more curious and forgot her frustration. Finally, she could resist it no longer and, pushing away the rock that blocked the cave's entrance, she went out to see Uzume dancing and delighting her audience. Amaterasu wanted a better view, so she emerged from the cave where her own image confronted her in a mirror that Uzume had placed there. Whilst Amaterasu gazed into the mirror, the spirits blocked the cave entrance and bound it with sacred rope, preventing Amaterasu from reentering the cave. With Amaterasu out of the cave, the sun rose again, and the world was saved. This is just one of Uzume's examples of her cunning and persuasive feats. And fortunately it was done for the greater good. The thing to bear in mind is that her energy is powerful, and it is up to you how you employ it in your life, and whether you can recognise when it is being used against you. Again, like every form of energy that we have access to and that we can manipulate, we make choices whether this energy fuels our light or serves to remove it.

Regaining Your Light with Uzume

The energy that a goddess like Uzume manifests can appear to you in two forms. The first is a most joyous, enchanting real-life individual who is full of fun and exuberance, with a smiling happy face—possibly as a child or a person who has very childlike qualities. In this form, her powers of persuasion will feel more like you are gently coaxed rather than pushed. And hints of spring flowers may linger in the air. The more beguiling energy may manifest in a person who stirs intense or buried emotions in you. You are drawn to them, against your better judgement. Sexual chemistry will spark, and you will find yourself throwing caution to the wind. And headier scents of jasmine or sandalwood can linger. It is worth noting that both manifestations of her energy provide opportunities, some prosperous and some more dangerous. But to best know which, you must come from inner stability, like so often when we are engaging with goddess energy through our emotional body.

To persuade others to your way of thinking or doing relies on the belief that the result will improve how things are now for you, or how you feel now first and foremost, and then belief that the other person or persons will also "see the light." Persuasion also relies on people believing that their current situation is no longer working for them; a much darker picture needs to be painted than perhaps it really is. But is this actually the case? Persuading a young child to hold your hand whilst crossing a busy road would be done without a second thought. But enforcing a belief on a person depicting their own faith in the worst possible light should be questioned. Who really stands to gain from this?

When we go about creating, experiencing, and living our lives, we do so most effectively when the other people in our lives are on the same page. However, helping someone see the light should not be undertaken if you have to plunge them into darkness first. Your goddess energy could be better used by being the example; then the choice is given to the other person as to what they wish to do, following in your footsteps or not. If you find yourself at the receiving end of a persuasive force, you will be more vulnerable if you have indeed gotten yourself into a dark hole, or if you have allowed yourself to become so drained that anything seems better than where you are or who you are right now. You will dwell on better things, happier times; you will be more open to temptations and far more easily persuaded to do something, anything, else, whether it is the right thing for you or not. Finding a way to hold our light and to be able to call upon it when we need can be of great help.

◎ Sun Meditation

An excellent way to reconnect with our inner light is to fuel it from the most magnificent light source we have in reach. Not only does engaging with the sun directly connect, awaken, and refuel us from within, it also lifts our spirits and nurtures our physical body with vitamins.

YOU WILL NEED:

* Open space outside, in direct sunlight, where you can be undisturbed for five to ten minutes; if you cannot go out, then somewhere indoors in front of an open, sunny window

Place yourself in full sunlight, so it can hit your skin. Remove shoes and socks if possible and get comfortable. Stand, feet shoulder-width apart, facing the sun. Feel the ground with your feet, curl your toes into the grass, soil, sand, carpet, or flooring and rock on your heels. Think about how it feels. Is it cold or warm underfoot? Is it soft, giving under your weight, or hard? Is it dry or moist? Now, with eyes closed, breathe in deeply, smelling the air. Notice how the air feels against your face and gently exhale. With your eyes still closed, tilt your face up to the sunlight. Feel the sun's warmth caressing your skin.

Now, visualise the sun as a conscious living being, a goddess. Raise your arms palms facing upwards. Uzume touches your hands and arms, warm and inviting. And she can hear you too. Now say, "Hail Sun, the giver of life! Hail the Day!"

Allow yourself to sense the energy, the light, all over your body and then penetrating your skin, from top to toe. At first, it is like gentle heat from the sunlight, and then as it goes deeper, it becomes a tingling sensation in your bones. Next, lower your arms and press your palms together at chest height, in front of your heart, promoting serenity and heart-centred focus.

Take in another deep breath, sensing the sunlight and goddess's presence on you and within you. During the next three slow, deliberate breaths, see that warm, pure light filling the hole that has been growing inside you. Feel this beautiful light penetrating every part of you, dispersing your doubts and your fears, anywhere your body or your mind needs attention, and let it gradually fill that place, as well as continuing to course through you. With every out-breath, visualise the release of any thoughts, feelings, or beliefs that no longer serve you. Keep doing this until you feel more complete and re-energised, and imagine the void within you now filled and every muscle and sinew released of tension and toxins. Know that something has changed, shifted within you. Rest your hands by your side and open your eyes. Give thanks and go about your day.

Tackling Temptation, Resolution Tips

You may well be wondering if it is really so easy to ignore temptation. Is resistance always for the greater good? And the answer is, of course, no, it is not. And you will, however hard you try to avoid it, succumb to temptation too. But by engaging in the practice of recognising your temptations, they lose their hold on you just a little. By giving your concerns a voice so that others have the opportunity to change, you may find your happiness is right where you are. And by allowing yourself to make changes and find ways to survive the moments of doubt, you take back control and gain greater insight and contentment. So the sooner we can discern between those things that serve us or tempt us and where our hearts genuinely reside, the more at ease we are with ourselves, so remember:

> When we create, we seldom do so alone or without impacting others. You need to bear this in mind to resist the temptation to lead others or be led by others against your will.

> Getting to grips with your creative energy, expressed via your emotions, opens up a world of possibilities in relationships where the balance of power is transformed, to shift it from a struggle for dominance to a haven of cooperation.

> Prepare yourself for the changes you wish to make by ensuring you are "grounded." Engaging the goddesses of temptation and persuasion can easily take you down a rabbit hole and keep you in a loop of succumbing to things that drain you of energy and self-worth.

When you encounter Deer Woman, you are reminded of the things you think you lack, the things you think you want or need, even other people. It will be impossible in life to avoid her at all times, so the sooner you learn how to manage temptation, what you can give way to and what to steer clear of, the easier your choices will become, and the more manageable the emotions Deer Woman stirs in you will be.

Make a habit of practising discernment as a way of understanding temptations in your life and managing them. The more you practise this, the easier it will become, until it is second nature to you.

Infidelity is most often linked to the darkest side of Deer Woman showing up in your life. Communication is a must; being honest for yourself and the others involved will yield the best outcome.

Persuasion is a necessary part of our journey, whether you are the one doing it or you find yourself in the grip of another's compelling tale. This is not to be confused with coercion; no act of persuasion should inflict physical or emotional harm.

The goddess Uzume used her many talents to bring warmth and light to the world, forgoing her sense of modesty and sensitivities. But as a consummate actress and master of her abilities, she knows just how this can play to others' strengths or weaknesses, reminding you to expend your energy wisely and sparingly.

Consider regular sun meditations to replenish your own body and soul, to rebalance your light and shadow, and to connect with the most abundant source of energy available to us. This meditation greatly assists you in your daily practices.

Chapter 4
Facing Fallout

The balance of power between men and women, between family members, within the workplace, within ourselves, between parents and their children, is more out of kilter now than perhaps it has ever been. So this is the time when gentle persuasion and subtle temptation have been pushed aside for their more aggressive versions to take hold. A time when you find yourself in one of two camps; you have either become the victim or the perpetrator, and you now have to combat the fallout of this choice. Look at why it occurs and what it takes to re-address it, starting with ourselves. Times will come in life when you cannot avoid harm, and you may even experience profound feelings of abandonment. Still, it is what we do in these dark times that defines and shapes us in order to not repeat the process if we are the perpetrators, nor to let the feeling overcome or consume us if we fall victim to this type of energy misuse.

Goddesses of the Seas

The stories of the goddess Sedna from Inuit mythology and the goddess Ran from Norse mythology deal with some of the darkest consequences of the misuse of power/energy, which manifest as abandonment and abuse. In this negative space, as if in a terrible storm at sea, you are battered by such a mix of emotions, with dark clouds all about you, desperately struggling under the weight of the water they carry. And it is also no surprise then to learn that both Sedna and Ran call the vast seas their home. There's something very sacred about the element of water; all belief systems understood its ability to cleanse, sustain, and transform, as well as its significance to all life on Earth. You, too, can harvest it and be given another way to bring yourself into alignment and harmony when needed.

◎ Creating Sacred Water

Sacred water (also referred to as "holy water") has many uses. It can cleanse a space of negative energies; splash or spray it over your focal point, or you can dab it on yourself or someone else as a blessing before ritual workings or meditation. Different types/sources of sacred water also carry specific properties. Using melted snow or rainwater adds strength. Seawater, considered sacred because of its salt content, is often used for cleansing and purification rituals. Rainwater can be used for rituals of purity, fertility, and abundance. Water collected during a storm is thought to be infused with powerful energy.

Morning dew can be used in rituals relating to beauty, healing, and rejuvenation. Many religious traditions believe that adding salt to sources of natural water can help ward off unfriendly spirits and entities. The following tips will equip you with the key ingredient for your sacred water ritual needs: the sacred water itself.

YOU WILL NEED:

* A vessel for the water; this can be a small bowl, a mug, or a small container
* Tablespoon of salt (ordinary table salt is acceptable)
* Access to tap water

To make sacred water for protection or cleansing, fill the vessel ¾ full with water. Dip your index finger into the water and say, *Behold this water, giver and carrier of life. I ask that it be blessed, purified, and made sacred. In the name of the goddess, in love, light, peace, and trust.* Next, cup your hand over the tablespoon of salt and say, *Behold the salt, preserver of life. I ask that it be blessed and purified. In the name of goddess, in love, light, peace, and trust.* Add a pinch of the salt to the water and mix them with your index finger, stirring in a clockwise direction. When thoroughly mixed, say, *For, as the water is sacred and as the salt is sacred, may their union be blessed, purified, and consecrated. In the name of goddess, by the power of the elements of earth, air, fire, and water, may this now be sacred water, to be used in goodness, love, light, peace, and trust. So mote it be.*

In addition to dispelling negative energy, you can use this type of sacred water by dabbing it on your skin for emotional stability or to make yourself more robust energetically. Start at the temples, then throat, heart chakra, wrists, and sacrum. By adding an item of silver to the sacred water, before leaving it in the moonlight, like a ring, bangle, or chain, the energy is infused in the metal, which then can be worn or carried with you.

Using sacred waters is not about quelling our emotions but channelling them for a more productive purpose. Feelings of hurt, anger, and resentment, for example, are accessible for a reason. They are a physical way of processing difficult experiences. These emotions are potent and can be used to create just as much as they may be used destructively. When we are able to channel these torrents of emotions more effectively, they can be very potent forces of positive change. It is all about coming to terms with the events that trigger these emotions and their reactions and allowing them to be expressed safely, rather than be suppressed and become a danger to ourselves and others around us. What you choose to do with your feelings determines whether they have a destructive or constructive effect. But continually suppressing negative emotions is like trying to hold back the floodgates, and eventually, this takes its toll.

Drowning Our Sorrows with Sedna

The great goddess of the sea and keeper of all its creatures, the Inuit goddess Sedna makes her presence felt via the icy, rough waters of the north. Whale calls resonate from deep below and above the water; waves rise and crash, crowned in a white spray. When great storms are brewing across the seas, it is Sedna calling out, "Come now, listen to me!" Sedna's energy can appear to you in two forms: as the once beautiful maiden, with flawless luminescent skin, large twinkling eyes, and soft lips framed by long, straight shining black hair; or as the abandoned, mutilated old goddess, her hair a black tangled wet mass, her face scarred, her eyes almost vacant, and just stumps for hands. But both these visions of her carry all the hurt and desperation that dwells in her heart, for she knows what is in store for you, and it is a painful, lonely journey. Her story is a warning of what can happen when you fall out with those you love by pursuing the wrong path. Sedna grew up in a small Inuit village with her father, who doted on her. Though they were happy, it was a harsh existence, especially during the bitterly cold winter months when food was hard to come by. But Sedna's father did all he could to ensure her comfort. Their home was modest, but Sedna had soft, warm pillows and ample hide blankets to keep her warm. They always had enough to drink and eat, and her father did all he could to keep her company. You could say he spoilt her, and he devoted his life to her, because she was all he had. But as Sedna grew older, her father's constant attention and praise moulded her into a self-centred young woman. She spent her days gazing upon her reflection, for she was beautiful, rather than helping her ailing father to hunt or fish, or to keep their home clean, or to cook or do anything to help herself or her father at all!

Eventually, the time came time for Sedna to marry and make a home for herself. Many men came to the village to offer Sedna a good home and treat her with respect and kindness, but she refused all her potential suitors, for she was far too beautiful for any of them and thought herself far too special to marry. Rather than engaging with anyone, she kept herself hidden away. But the winters grew harsher each year, food grew scarce, and Sedna's father feared for her future as he struggled to provide for two. He believed the only way they could both survive was for Sedna to marry, and he decided to order her to marry the next man that would ask. Because Sedna was so incredibly beautiful, he knew this would not take long, and even though he knew he could not provide for them both any longer, his heart weighed heavy at the thought of her leaving.

It wasn't long before a heavily cloaked stranger came to the village, and having met Sedna, was taken by her beauty and asked for her hand in marriage. Sedna unhappily followed her father's orders and reluctantly accepted. Though neither Sedna nor her father could see the stranger's face beneath his hood, the fact that he promised her a life of riches and all the food she could eat made Sedna's father happy that his daughter would be looked after and that he could survive. That night the stranger drugged Sedna's water. When she awoke in the morning, she drank her water, bid a sad farewell to her father and, en route to her new home, passed out as the drugs took hold.

Sedna awoke to a howling wind, bird calls in the distance, and the faint sound of the sea. As she opened her eyes, she realised she was on a large cliff overlooking the sea. Beside her was not a cloaked man but a large black raven with an immense wingspan and glassy black eyes staring at her. Sedna's heart broke, and tears tumbled from her eyes as she cried inconsolably. With no soft pillows or warm hide blankets or boiled water to drink, or anyone for company, her life was a misery. The raven did not pity such a self-centred girl, and though his nest was large, he left her with only a few feathers for protection against the cutting wind. But Sedna was exposed to all the elements; the wind cut her bare skin and tangled her long hair. Every night she cried in pain and misery, praying that her father would come and rescue her. Her desperate, piercing cries carried on the wind to her old village, and her father, feeling guilty for forcing her to marry a stranger, decided he would try to find and rescue his daughter.

Following the cries that so tugged at his heart, he paddled his kayak out to sea and was shocked to discover his daughter trapped alone high on a cliff above him. He called to her to jump down into his kayak. Sedna jumped down into the kayak and made herself comfortable, wrapped in hides and furs, while her father paddled home as quickly as he was able. Sedna's father had been paddling for a couple of hours when Sedna spotted something black in the sky coming towards them. She was struck with fear at the thought that it might be the raven coming for her and pleaded for her father to paddle harder. However, her father was growing very tired, and so instead of continuing to paddle or even paddling faster, he stopped to regain his strength.

It wasn't long before the calm sea began to stir, and the kayak pitched heavily in the choppy waves. As the waves grew larger, Sedna and her father looked behind them and there in all his intimidating glory was the giant raven, flapping his enormous black wings on the surface of the sea. The commotion caused the waters around them to become more turbulent and the kayak to rock more violently. The raven was furious that Sedna had tried to escape him and that her father was helping her in her treachery. He flapped his wings even more vigorously, and the kayak was on the verge of tipping. Sedna's father panicked in fear for his own life now, believing that he was wrong to help his daughter; he called out to the raven, "Have her!" Sedna looked at her father in disbelief, and at that moment, he raised his paddle and walloped her with it so ferociously that it threw Sedna overboard.

Sedna hit the icy waters and cried out to her father for help, then screamed at the raven to ward him off. Desperate to live, she grabbed the kayak and tried to scramble back in. But her father raised his paddle again and brought it down on her fingers. They were so cold they had almost frozen, and the paddle broke them clean off, floating down to the bottom of the sea where it is said they transformed into seals, otters, and walruses. The raven, seeing Sedna's attempts to escape again, continued in his frenzy to flap his wings and unsteady the kayak. Sedna now tried to wrap her arms around the end of the kayak so as not to drown, and again the paddle came down on her, snapping off her near frozen hands. They, too, floated to the bottom of the sea to transform into porpoises and whales. Without any fight left in her, Sedna fell back into the sea and sank to the bottom. She was now transformed into a great sea goddess.

Now legend has it the goddess Sedna is responsible for all storms at sea and that her rage and resentment at her father's betrayal is the reason why all Inuit hunters respect the sea so much. It is said that only a special kind of person, one who has mastered their personal power and who can commune with the elements, like a shaman, is worthy of Sedna, and could swim down to her to comb her long black her and, in so doing, calm the stormy sea. This level of respect for this great sea goddess is why an Inuit hunter drops water into his prey's mouth; it is a sign of respect to show gratitude to Sedna for allowing the hunter to feed his family.

The emotions stirred up when we feel wronged by those we trusted, loved, or relied on can be devastating. We can turn to rage and resentment, and set about a lifelong rocky path of victimhood, seeing all things that do not go the way we thought or want as a personal slight on us, that it is always other people's fault that our own lives are not what we feel we wanted or deserved. You may feel abandoned, but that does not mean you need to abandon your responsibility to yourself and your actions forever. Sedna's power can affect you if you only focus on the story from one perspective.

All along her journey, before she transformed, Sedna had opportunities to take control of her circumstances and make different choices. She always had the chance to look past her reflection at the world about her; she could have helped her father; she could have chosen a husband; she could have appreciated her own life more. But this becomes increasingly difficult when you allow negativity to build up and take hold. What can help is to off-load these feelings to make room for more positive energy to thrive and see more clearly what is possible for you. The next ritual can help you do this and embrace Sedna's goddess energy's strengths rather than dwell on her tragic past.

◎ DISSOLUTION OF SORROWS RITUAL

YOU WILL NEED:

* A quiet space, preferably outside in nature, where you will be undisturbed
* A small handheld bell to cleanse the space
* A small bowl of freshly prepared sacred water
* A sheet of rice paper
* A stick or twig for stirring (ideally gather it from your outside space)

Once you have found your "sacred space," the place where you can practise this ritual without being disturbed, you need to energetically "clear" the space. Do this by taking your bell to proceed by cleansing the four directions (full details of this can be found in Chapter 1 as part of "Creating a Simple Focal Point"). When you are done, put your cleansing tool to one side and now, with your bowl and rice paper and twig, sit in the middle of the space facing west (the direction of transformation), and put the bowl and twig on the ground before you. Next, close your eyes and take three deep breaths in through the nose and exhale through the mouth. Gently open your eyes and continue to breathe steadily.

Allow each emotional trauma that you have been holding to rise to the surface individually on the in-breath, and as it does, tear off a little piece of rice paper and place it in the bowl of water as you breathe out. As each trauma, hurt, or sorrow rises to the surface, don't dwell on it; just think of it attaching itself to the little piece of rice paper you have torn off and placed in the bowl. Take as much time as you need, steadily and calmly. You will probably find that you have either more rice paper left over than "sorrows," or you have more sorrows coming to the fore than bits of rice paper. Both are fine; if you have rice paper left over, just lay it down on the ground beside you. If you have more "sorrows" than rice paper, allow each sorrow to take root in the water on the out-breath where they will dissolve with the rest.

Now, take your stick and begin to stir the dissolving rice paper in the sacred water. As you do so say, "Transform my sorrows, my hurts, and pain, make new in me from which they came, sacred waters I turn to thee, pass them to the earth and set me free." Stir and repeat till the rice paper has fully dissolved, then taking your bowl, stand up and pour the contents onto the ground of the nearest shrub or tree. Earth is a great transformer of energy. The soil absorbs your "sorrows" and in so doing begins the recycling process of that energy, then it is taken up by the tree and shrub roots as energy for growth, and finally, what is left is released into the air as pure, neutral energy.

Practising this ritual as often as you feel necessary gets you out into a natural healing environment, which is uplifting. Being embraced by nature in this way, the grass under your feet, the sun on your face or the wind in your hair, hearing bird song or a chime in the breeze, all combine to connect you to the source of all life. It reminds you that you are indeed part of a greater living entity and that you are never truly alone or abandoned. Knowing that you can use this ritual to release and transform your sorrows may help you feel less hopeless when an argument or fallout occurs. You can also do this ritual with the person with whom you have argued, as a way of cleansing the energy between you, starting from a clean slate, so to speak. It is very beneficial to be around people who are able to release their feelings productively too.

But thus far, we have only really addressed the emotional side of being the victim of fallout. You may not immediately think of associating playing the victim with the creative forces of your inner goddess. Still, it is a potent weapon in its own right and it can be extremely destructive when unleashed on others with the intention to harm. As has been said, goddess energy is just that, energy in its rawest creative form, neither positive nor negative. It is how we harness it and what we create with it that determines when it becomes something positive and helpful or negative and detrimental. There are genuine victims in life, and you may well become the victim of circumstances beyond your control, but you don't need to stay there long or use it against others; that is your choice and your authentic power working positively.

Just as Sedna's story highlights that there is always an opportunity to change a situation and therein change how you are feeling, it is also a reminder that if you continue to use emotions like entitlement, anger, and resentment to feed your creative desire, the outcome will always be more of the same. And just as the tides of the oceans that play host to the goddesses of this chapter, it is a two-way thing. Facing fallout will come to you just as impactfully when you are the one to cause the tidal wave. You have to face the perpetrator in you, the harbinger of all that ill will, because only then can you go about managing that creative part of yourself. It is time now to reveal the goddess that encompasses this aspect of your emotional makeup; meet the goddess for whom nothing is ever enough.

What Lies Beneath

It is said we know more about outer space than we do about our oceans. More stories are written about monstrous creatures that dwell in deep waters than those on land, as we seldom know what we are truly capable of when pushed to our limits—what monsters will surface? You are not expected to handle everything all the time, for life is a great teacher. You may only encounter the next goddess's energy under extreme duress, but awareness is a valuable tool. In Norse mythology, the great goddess Ran ruled the seas. She was a personification of its power, majesty, turbulence, and mystery. With her jotunn husband, Aegir, she had nine stunning daughters, who were referred to as the spirits of the waves or the nine billow maidens. Ran's naked, greeny-blue iridescent skin camouflaged her perfectly as she moved in the sea depths, her long dark hair flowing behind her like ribbons of black seaweed. She had no equal in her domain and was adored by her family. But this was not enough for Ran. Her name means "to plunder," and her insatiable appetite for getting what she wanted would result in her spending her days catching sailors at will in her giant silvery net. Once in her net, she would pull them down to their watery graves, bedding them and holding them there in limbo.

But none ever dared challenge or question Ran, not even the other deities, who were more inclined to join her in great feasts to stay on her good side. Mortal sailors would sometimes pay tribute to Ran before they embarked on their journeys to raid or trade. They hoped that these treasures would please her and that she would grant them safe passage at sea. Fear is what fed the sacrifices to her, fear is the energy they carried as she took them, and misery is the energy that lingers with them in the depths. Ran is consequentially a goddess that, as powerful as she might seem, is sustained by the fear, anguish, and pain of her conquests and the constant offerings by those seeking to avoid her wrath. These feelings are not fulfilling, and therefore the emotions that Ran invokes are never satisfying, nor do they bring you any real, lasting pleasure in life.

When Ran's energy presents itself, it is often through a heightened emotional drive to take what you want from others at all costs. And in this context, it is about bending the will of others to suit your own. It is that energy that you engage with when making threats or twisting the truth to get who or what you want. Her power's most abusive form makes you see a red mist when you should be keeping a cool head, and tends to arise quickly and without warning. In toddlers who throw a tantrum or teenagers who fire verbal abuse, it is generally not meant to hurt the other person but get a reaction. However, in women, this energy can be especially cruel, withholding affection or love. And if you find yourself at the receiving end, it is like being hit by a wall of water, all-engulfing, throwing you off balance, not knowing which way is up, and you struggle to see a way out.

Navigating Loss

Navigating turbulent emotional seas takes its toll. You can be left feeling anxious, worried, depressed, grieving, stagnant, fearful, ashamed, overwhelmed, and many other energy-sapping emotions at times in life. And at times, these feelings can linger and take root for much longer than we would desire or is healthy. How wonderful it would be to have such self-mastery of our emotions to be able to sense, process, release, and integrate our emotions at will. But that is not the real world in which most of us dwell. If we are lucky, we look for or are shown ways to steer ourselves into tranquil harbours. For some years now, I have found physical actions, no matter how simple, help considerably to manage emotions, especially coming out of the other side of difficult or traumatic events.

My first husband of just three years committed suicide out of the blue when I was 26 years old. I do believe that if I had known about the tools, exercises, and rituals that I share with you in this book, much of what happened in the hours, days, weeks, and then subsequent months after his death, and much of what I felt, would have been managed very differently. I would have probably made different choices, said other things, and looked to take more control of my life at the time, and spoken out more in a positive, constructive manner; I might have been spared much self-doubt and backlash.

I was a bit like the goddess Sedna, focusing only on what I had lost rather than all I still had. My drive for revenge and my hatred for those I saw responsible at the time meant I could easily have given into lawless actions, none of which would have changed the fact that my best friend was gone. It took me a year, but I rebuilt my life, kept a roof over my head, and even allowed my heart to open. But the pain of that loss at times, that sense of abandonment, still niggle from time to time, decades later. I have always loved being in nature, particularly near open water, and now love working with all the elements, so that is why I have chosen the next ritual for you.

◎ CAST IN STONE RITUAL

Trying to deal with anger or frustration in the heat of the moment is difficult. You could physically remove yourself and your energy from that situation, but that does not address the feelings you have, and the tension that has been created in your physical and emotional body. This is when the elements come into their own. The most stabilising is the element of earth, and it is so beneficial to work with when you're left feeling stuck. Being weighed down by emotion can be greatly relieved by giving it over to Mother Earth, whose forces can transmute it with ease. In opposition often is the element of water; however, it can also be a great accelerator of energy work and act as a conduit, providing almost instant relief to the physical body.

YOU WILL NEED:

* Small basin for a foot bath
* A cup or a small bowl of sacred water (see "Creating Sacred Water Ritual")
* Epsom salts or sea salt
* A few drops of essential oil; either vetiver, chamomile, or ylang-ylang
* A selection of small stones or pebbles
* A quiet space in nature where you will not be disturbed, ideally near to open water

We begin this ritual with the selective gathering of stones and pebbles that call to you in preparation. Going for a short walk in nature, along a riverbed or bank, along the sea, are ideal to find them. But equally, you may find the pebble you seek in a wooded area, in a field, or just in your own garden. When you are doing this, for each stone you pick up, transfer a negative feeling to it as you hold it. Use one stone for each emotion, person, or situation that has made you angry or resentful or bitter. Collect about half a dozen or so in a bag and keep them next to your bed overnight. Set the intention that they absorb your difficult emotions, or you can write them on the rocks instead with biodegradable markers.

Now place the stones carefully in your basin, evenly across the bottom, fill your basin with warm water, and add the salts and the cup of sacred water. Add your essential oils. Next, place your bare feet in the bowl to rest on top of the stones. Allow your feet to move over the surface of the stones, sensing how they feel. Now visualise your pain, hurt, or other difficult emotions being drawn out from your body and into the water to infuse the stones. See these emotions being pulled out of your body by the cleansing water and held in the stones. Watch as these emotions drain out of your feet and into the stones. When you feel ready, drain your foot bath, give thanks to the water element, then take the basin outside and place the stones near a tree or shrub for the elements of earth and air to slowly unlock and transmute the energy of the emotions within.

You can do this regularly, if you would like, using the same stones if it helps (be sure to allow at least forty-eight hours for the energy to be released), or you can make this a special part of each month or season. Letting go of emotions that feel unhelpful to us, or feel like they're holding us back, is essential to our wellbeing. Trying to suppress these emotions when they arise or get stuck is not the same as managing them. Releasing emotions is about experiencing them to serve a purpose but not to the point that they dictate your life. Sometimes, these emotions get stuck, and that's okay because we have the tools to release them.

Elemental Turbulence

All ancient cultures revere the elements of nature. Water has played a key part in this chapter of the four common elements of nature; it is the element associated with our emotional body. And as our physical bodies primarily consist of that element, too, it is no surprise that this element plays the central role in our relationships' ebb and flow. The element of water permeates our physical environment also. It exists in its purest forms as bodies of water: the oceans, rivers, and lakes. It permeates the air in the form of rain, mist, and dew, and it also takes solid form as snow and ice. To our planet, water is as vital as it is to your body and mine.

Water is the "carrier" element, and to a degree, it can also exacerbate our emotions, helping them expand and flow beyond normal reach. But like all things created from Source, from universal energy, there is no bias to create a negative or positive outcome; all it does is offer a neutral space to plant our intent, our emotional energy. And the more we feed that space, that calm, deep pool of creativity, with stable, balanced emotions or inspiration and positive ideas, the more those things grow and expand, and something truly remarkable can manifest. However, the opposite is also possible. Feeding that same pool with aggressive, vengeful, negative ideas and intent, the more those things multiply, and the calm pool becomes a raging body of turbulent choppy water where it is impossible to manifest anything constructive at all.

The other primary elements of nature, earth, air, and fire, play their part in our emotional development and support, just as they are also integral to our planet's well-being and energetic balance. The element of earth is a great stabiliser, the foundations on which we stand both physically and emotionally, and the holder of energy and emotion to then release it in a manner that we can cope with better. It also is the engine that drives the transformation of our emotions and the energy they create. It is the element that best helps to balance the aspect of water within.

The element of air is the great carrier of our emotions. Just as water is held in mist, raindrops, and snow, having been first collected in one place to be released later in another, far and wide, so too the energy of our emotions can reach out far and wide and impact others without our knowledge. The often unpredictable element of air acts as a reminder of the potential within all of us and offers an abundance of "thinking space" to allow those inspired to make plans and realise their dreams, their hopes, and even come up with solutions to problems of the heart or mind. To connect with this element, get out into nature as often as you can, as far away from built-up areas as possible, and in all weathers. Experience the rain on your face, the wind in your hair, notice the birds in flight or insects hovering in the air, and above all, breathe it in.

To complete the circle is the element of fire whose interaction with water on an emotional level can be intense but yield almost instantaneous results. Fire can bring a situation to a head when it appears to be stagnating or festering. This plays out when people finally deal with the facts of a situation rather than the feelings. Sometimes no matter how emotionally invested we are in something, there may be no alternative other than to let go. For example, you love the house you live in, but it is too big, no longer affordable, or too far away from your new job, and so no matter how you feel about the place, the facts dictate that you must move. Coming to terms with the idea that you can feel differently, that you can see beyond the here and now, and believe in a different outcome to the one you think is inevitable and fills you with dread will in itself change things for the better.

◎ CALLING TO THE QUEENS EXERCISE

What follows now is an exercise chosen for you to provide a simple yet effective way to engage with all the elements to navigate stormy emotional seas. Or it can be used more regularly to keep an even keel and help to minimise the fallout from any emotional situations that arise. As with all the "resolutions" in this book, the more you engage with this exercise, the better prepared you will be when a situation arises that has the potential to overwhelm you or sink your mood.

YOU WILL NEED:

* A quiet space where you can sit at a table undisturbed for ten to fifteen minutes
* A bell or rattle to "clear" the space
* A deck of playing cards (or any divination deck that contains elemental representations)

Having found your quiet space, you need to energetically "clear" it using your bell or rattle. These handy little tools clear or cleanse by agitating and moving the energy with sound vibration. Set your intention, which is to create a clear space for your energy work. Now ring the bell or shake the rattle over the table. A tip to make sure you cover your working area is to sit at the table and shake your bell or rattle up and down in a vertical line in front of you and then from left to right horizontally, crossing the vertical line, finishing off with three circular motions to take in the outer rim of the area you have created with your vertical and horizontal lines. But this is just a guide, and as long as you "agitate" the space above the table where you will be working, that is fine too; remember, it is the intention that is most important.

Next, from your deck of cards, take out the queens of each set. Now imagine the points of a compass displayed in front of you on the table. Take the Queen of Spades and place her face up where the direction of north would be and say, *Hail and welcome goddess of earth, I call to you now to draw upon your wisdom and understanding of all that has been to help calm the stormy seas of emotion within me.* Next, take the Queen of Clubs and place her face up where the direction of east would be and say, *Hail and welcome goddess of air, I call to you now to draw upon your intent, focus, and ingenuity to spark my creativity and help me channel the emotions within me.* Now, take the Queen of Diamonds and place her face up where the direction of south would be and say, *Hail and welcome goddess of fire, I call to you now to draw upon your passion and intensity for manifesting anew to help transform the stormy seas of emotion within me.*

Finally, take the Queen of Hearts and place her face up where the direction of west would be and say, *Hail and welcome goddess of water, I call to you now to turn to your sisters. Heed the wisdom of the earth; no need to exhaust yourself whipping up a storm, let the waters settle and calm. Allow your focus to fall away from negativity, sorrow, and anger and instead channel emotions that are uplifting and positive and take inspiration from the air. Finally, allow your heart to be warmed by the passion of fire and know that together balance is restored, and in time, all will be well again. Blessed be.*

Now take a good look at the queens before you on the table. Next, in no particular order, gather them together in your dominant hand and rest the other hand on top. Now close your eyes, and in your mind's eye, visualise the goddesses of the elements coming together as one, restoring the balance within you, quelling the emotions that have overridden your sense of right and wrong. Hold this image in your mind's eye for a few moments longer and as you take three deep breaths, draw in the sense of calm and exhale any remnants of anger, injustice, abandonment, or sorrow. When you feel ready, open your eyes and go about your day.

Our emotions act as guides and signals. And they are the best way we know to express our very being. They can, however, be easily influenced and manipulated by circumstance and other people. However, having a handle on your emotions and how they can be triggered is an ongoing study. But you can learn what triggers your most turbulent emotions, and you can put into place things to balance your emotions. Understanding them in an elemental form means that whichever type of feeling is dominant, you can employ three other elements to minimise the impact. When you are at the beck and call of the goddesses Sedna and Ran, it is not a time to feel helpless or angry but to look to the opportunities that can come from reaching this point. The goddesses have great strength, allure, and persuasive power; you need to use that for manifesting something new, something better, something that, rather than hold you down, will allow you to move forward—to ride the wave.

Wave Rider

From fallout, from the arguments, shouting matches, or more destructive encounters, multiple options will unfold before you. You may only see one outcome initially, but even that outcome need not be permanent. You can dive deep and reside with Sedna or Ran for a while, but then rise to the surface and be free from sorrow; you can choose to make something better or begin something new. Appreciate that what you have gone through is to strengthen your resolve, not to weaken it. Understand what the goddesses want to teach you. Sedna's struggle to cling to the kayak might have been made just based on a desire to stay alive in that instance; I like to think she finally understood what was important in life. Though not saving her mortal life, this profound realisation transformed her into a sea goddess for whom all have respect, and she better appreciates the place she protects.

One would hope you wouldn't need to lose a limb to appreciate what is good in your life, nor that you would need to resort to bedding any man that comes your way just to exude your power or dominance. But it is a sad fact that people can self-destruct mentally and physically when dragged low enough. You don't want to self-harm to feel alive, or dive so deep that you believe your death is the only and best outcome. These are extreme but not uncommon results of a considerable imbalance in our emotions when we are desperate. Moving forward or riding that wave may even be about admitting you were wrong. It isn't always an end to something. Remember, you cannot avoid the battle, but how deep you are taken below the surface is entirely up to you. Facing fallout is not about drowning in the sea of your emotions but being resilient enough to stay afloat and swim to the shore.

Facing Fallout, Resolution Tips

In times of imbalance or disagreement, the choices that feel right can be fuelled by fear, anger, and resentment. When you willingly choose to succumb to the more destructive emotions in a relationship, your creative energy will fuel a troubled heart or mind, so please consider:

> Testing times are inevitable, and though we may have no say when they happen or what the result will be, we do have a choice in how badly the fallout impacts our emotional state. We can choose to suffer less by employing ways to manage our emotions, especially the most negative or destructive.

Develop an understanding and appreciation of the element of water. Know why it holds such power over us and its significance in our being by looking at the role it plays in our bodies, our beliefs and religions, and our environment and planet as a whole.

Make a habit of creating and having to hand sacred or holy water to use in your ritual work. Explore how this sacred water can best work for you.

Please become familiar with the levels of discord or disruption in your life and their subsequent escalating levels of fallout. Recognising these and managing the emotions they invoke in you can prevent a petty disagreement from becoming an outright slanging match or worse.

The goddess Sedna's story reminds us that we need to appreciate what we have and make positive efforts to engage in our journey rather than take a "me, me, me" approach that can leave us in a very precarious position. It is a tale of karma; essentially, what goes around comes around

Ritual work helps connect us physically, energetically, and spiritually to our intention, outcome, the actual tools we use, and the environment we do the ritual in. Dissolution of Sorrows is a ritual that engages you in physical activity and engages the elements to help you authentically realise your intention.

There are always two sides to everything, and where Sedna plays the victimhood card, the goddess Ran is a manifestation of the perpetrator in you. Understanding how Ran manifests in our lives, and how we feel in her energy, helps us determine what action we should take or how to completely mitigate her energy.

To "cast in stone" demonstrates the collective power of nature for helping us energetically, emotionally, and physically. It also requires care on our part in how we use these tools, and adds to our reverence for them and our desire to aid our wellbeing.

Exploring the other primary elements' role when dealing with emotional fallout emphasises the importance of a holistic view, not only when working with resolutions but also of life itself and our experience. "Calling to the Queens" is a simple but effective way to do this and to restore balance.

You cannot avoid conflict all the time; sometimes you will be on the receiving end, or you will instigate it, but effectively managing the feelings that arise is the first step to creating something positive from that experience.

CHAPTER 5
Shut Up or Put Up

S ometimes we will clash with others' ideas, opinions, and way of life. But when things are not right for long enough, two paths become clear; one is the path of "compliance": you say nothing, shut off, and shut up. You give over to the will of another or a situation as it is and become a passenger in your journey. The other path can be more chaotic or destructive for those around you, as you put up a fight for what you feel is right. You are in the driving seat to take control and venture into the unknown. These pathways are represented by two opposing goddess energies and are revealed by the lessons of their myths.

Goddesses in Opposition

So much in this life, where we all are on the collective journey, is like a balancing act between extreme ends of the ideal situation, like our need to consume from the planet vs. our need to care for it. The stories of Persephone of Greek mythology and Kali of Hindu myth exemplify this struggle. It can feel very much that you are being forced to take a "side" to survive rather than thrive in the middle ground. When dealing with the energies involved in either choosing to let life happen to you or to break and remake your life, a significant number of vulnerabilities, fears, and temptations can make either choice damaging in the long term.

Being permanently under the influence of either one of the energies is not ideal; however, both present great learning and growth opportunities, changing your perception and doing things for the better. We all recognise that there are times when it is nice to take a backseat in life and let others take on the responsibilities, pressures, and decision making for you. As a child and young adult, this is not at all uncommon and often necessary. But there is a fine line between choosing to and being forced to against your will or better judgement. As you develop your sense of being and purpose, the desire to make decisions should be encouraged. We all need to have the confidence to stand in our power.

Twin Spheres of Support

The resolutions on offer in this book are not about preventing life from happening to you. They are not about shielding you from every ill, danger, or disaster, but about understanding that you can cope and get through them in a way that offers some enrichment and encouragement in your life experience, rather than have it be nothing but pain or confusion. Already, as a person able to afford the time and energy to read this book, you have an advantage that so many other people in life don't. Make even more of all that potential, of all you have been through already, and of all that is yet to come. The following pair of meditations have been included to help you restore energetic balance by either drawing you away from unhealthy over-compliance and total reliance on others, or by bringing you down from the dizzy heights of reckless over-control and a complete disregard for others.

◎ Sphere of Clarity Meditation

A meditation for "clarity" helps you see the bigger picture, the truth of what is going on in your life or a particular situation. It will help you identify what is best for you, your way ahead. Importantly, it will help you see what you should be doing, and how you should be investing your energy to see and manifest it more positively, rather than waiting for things to happen for, or to, you.

You will need:

* A quiet space where you will be undisturbed for twenty to twenty-five minutes
* A cushion or mat to sit on (if required)
* A small cup of sacred water
* A few drops of peppermint essential oil

*   A clear quartz crystal gemstone, small enough to
    be held in one hand

Ensure you are wearing loose clothing and find your quiet space; it can be inside or outside, up to you. Sit down on the floor or ground so that you are comfortable and warm, with your cup of sacred water, essential oil, and gemstone placed in front of you within easy reach. Prepare your water by putting a few drops of the peppermint essential oil in it and stir it around with your index finger. The peppermint oil helps to open the capillaries under the skin, allowing the energy you are about to call upon to be more easily infused and circulated.

Now raise the cup to your face, close your eyes, and take three deep breaths. Open your eyes and place the cup down in front of you. Dip your index finger into the cup and draw a line of the sacred peppermint water across your brow, from one temple to the other. Dip your finger into the cup again, and reaching round, draw a line across the back of the neck at the base (on the skin). Finally, dip your finger into the cup and draw a line across the inside of the opposite wrist, and then rub the inside of both wrists together. Pick up and hold the crystal in your dominant hand.

Close your eyes and notice the sensation of the water on your body; it might feel cooling and tingling. Take another three deep breaths and notice any sounds around you, even the silence; notice any smells; let both of these sensations come to you and then pass as you continue to breathe steadily. How does the crystal feel in your hand? Is it cold or warm, smooth, or edged? Again, let these things come to mind and then pass. Continue to breathe steadily, and with your mind's eye, focus on the sensations and image of the crystal in your hand. Imagine the crystal now beginning to resonate in your hand and releasing the white light energy that fills your hand. This light represents pure, rejuvenating energy that illuminates your truth.

Next, imagine the light gently expanding with each in-breath until the light encases you, holding you in this place of clarity. Just reside in this light, and let any thoughts that come to mind be acknowledged and released. Allow this light to infuse your very being. You may begin to have ideas or feelings that highlight what is not suitable for you that cause pain and dissatisfaction. Don't analyse; instead, allow the thoughts to be acknowledged, infused with the light, and then pass. Breathing normally, dwell in the presence of this healing light for as long as you desire or feel comfortable.

When you are ready, imagine the sphere of light retracting slowly to the crystal in your hand. Open your eyes, stretch your arms and legs, wiggling your fingers before you get up. Taking your crystal and cup, clear things away and go about your day. This meditation can be undertaken whenever you need invigoration, or you can make it part of a weekly or monthly routine to help maintain clarity and the energy to do the things your newfound insight reveals.

◎ Sphere of Calm Meditation

The companion meditation that follows is most appropriate in times of complete opposition to the above; in other words, when you are the orchestrator of everything, every thought, action, and reaction is going on not just in your life, but also in the lives of those around you. This heightened state of involvement can be self-evident: lots of shouting instructions, nagging, doing jobs that other people should be doing, almost at a manic level, like multiple limbs on the go all at once. Or it may take a more subtle form: constantly suggesting to people what they might do, what they might think or say, no less manic, just a lot quieter.

You will need:

* A quiet space where you can sit undisturbed for twenty to twenty-five minutes

* A cushion or mat to sit on (if required)

* A small cup of sacred water

* A few drops of lavender essential oil

* A black obsidian gemstone small enough to be held in one hand

Ensure you are wearing loose clothing and find your quiet space; it can be inside or outside, up to you. Sit down on the floor or ground so that you are comfortable and warm, with your cup of sacred water, essential oil, and gemstone placed in front of you within easy reach. Prepare your water by putting a few drops of the lavender essential oil in it and stir it around with your index finger. The lavender oil helps open capillaries under the skin, allowing the energy you are about to call upon to be more easily infused and circulated. Now raise the cup to your face, close your eyes, and take five deep breaths.

Open your eyes and place the cup down in front of you. Dip your index finger into the cup and draw a line of the sacred lavender water across your breastbone over the heart (on the skin). Dip your finger into the cup again, and, reaching round to the base of your spine, rub a small circle on the area (on the skin). Finally, dip your finger into the cup and draw a line across the inside of the opposite wrist, and then rub the inside of both wrists together. Pick up and hold the obsidian stone in your dominant hand.

Now sitting there, close your eyes and notice the sensation of the water on your body; it might feel warm and tingly. Take another five deep breaths and notice any sounds around you, even if it is the sound of silence; notice any smells; let both of these sensations come to you and then pass as you continue to breathe deeply and steadily. Notice how the obsidian feels in your hand; is it cold or warm, smooth, or can you feel edges? Again, let these things come to mind and then pass. Continue to breathe steadily, and with your mind's eye, focus on the sensations and image of the crystal in your hand. Imagine the crystal now beginning to resonate in your hand and releasing the nurturing dark blue light that fills your hand. This light represents pure, nurturing energy that quells your racing thoughts.

Imagine the dark light gently expanding with each in-breath until the light encases you, holding you in this place of sanctuary. Just reside in this place and let any thoughts that come to mind be acknowledged and released. Allow this energy to infuse your very being. You may begin to have ideas or feelings that highlight what you fear losing, that cause you anger and frustration. Don't analyse; instead, allow the thoughts to come in, be acknowledged, held in the dark light, and then pass. Breathing normally, dwell in the presence of this healing space for as long as you desire or feel comfortable.

When you are ready, imagine the sphere of dark light retracting slowly back to the obsidian in your hand. Open your eyes, stretch out your arms and legs, wiggling fingers before you get up. Taking your crystal and cup, clear things away and go about your day. This meditation can be undertaken whenever you feel you need to release tensions or slow your thoughts, or make it part of a weekly or monthly routine to help maintain calm and release the tight grip on matters you need not control.

It is always much more productive and less stressful, I find, to approach any type of goddess energy work from as "balanced" a standpoint as possible. Being at a midpoint, so to speak, means you have far less distance to cover to reach your goal than if you have to come at it from the furthest point away. That being said, I would suggest if you are more of a "control freak" who, like me, has to be at the wheel rather than a "passenger," then focus on feeling comfortable with the Spere of Calm Meditation first. And if you are the opposite, then I urge you to seek clarity through the Sphere of Clarity Meditation first.

And now it is time to introduce the Greek goddess of the Underworld, Persephone, whose story is as much about what other people do as it is about what she does not. From her story, we can see the power of strong emotional ties and how these ties can bind rather than liberate all involved.

Being Taken for a Ride

According to Greek mythology, Persephone, the beautiful and charming young daughter of Zeus and Demeter, attracted many gods' attention, including the much older god of the Underworld, Hades. His years of living in the dark with only the shadows of the dead for company had turned his heart to stone, but as soon as he caught sight of the gentle Persephone, it began to soften. However, Demeter, who adored her only daughter, could not bear the idea of losing her child to any god, ever, and so kept all men away. So when Hades asked Demeter to marry her daughter, Demeter was enraged and vowed no one, not even the great god Hades, brother of Zeus, would ever take Persephone from her. But Hades, struck by the feelings even just Persephone's image evoked in him, made it his mission to have her as his wife.

One day, while Persephone was picking flowers in a valley, she noticed the most exquisite narcissus she had ever seen. As she bent down to pick it, the earth beneath her opened up, allowing Hades on his chariot drawn by black horses to grab Persephone and take her back down into the Underworld before it seemed anyone noticed she was gone. However, there had been two witnesses, Zeus and the god of the sun, Helios. Even though his daughter was abducted, Zeus said nothing because he didn't want conflict with his brother. And Helios decided it was better just to keep quiet because it was none of his concern.

Demeter was distraught and wandered the earth looking for her daughter until the goddess Hekate advised her to speak to Helios. Helios took pity on Demeter, who pleaded for his help, and told her what he had seen. Demeter wanted to take revenge on Hades, her anger now at boiling point. But Helios pointed out that perhaps it was not so awful for Persephone to be such a powerful goddess in her own right as the queen of the Underworld. All her needs would be catered to by Hades, who was so taken by her. But this only made things worse as Demeter believed that Hades was not the right husband for her sweet daughter. And when she discovered that Zeus knew too and said nothing, she decided to punish all the gods.

Demeter gave up her duties as the goddess of harvest and fertility, and the earth began to dry up, causing crops to fail, plants to wither, and animals to die, resulting in untold misery. The audible anguish of the suffering people reached Zeus in Olympus, and he realised that the people would all die if he didn't do something to quell Demeter's wrath. So Zeus told Demeter that if she could prove Hades was holding Persephone against her will, Hades would have to give her up. But Hades got wind of this, and knowing his young bride was miserable, he fed her a few pomegranate seeds. This food of the Underworld, when consumed, would create a false longing to be there. And as it happened, when she stood in front of Zeus and was asked where she wanted to live, Persephone said she wanted to remain with Hades.

On hearing these words, Demeter accused Hades of tricking her daughter and threatened to kill everyone on earth by refusing to make it fertile again. So Zeus decided that Persephone would spend six months with her husband in the Underworld and the other six months with her mother on Olympus to end this feud. Reluctantly, Hades and Demeter accepted this. And so the lovely Persephone became the wife of Hades and queen of the Underworld, spending autumn and winter below the earth, and spring and summer above it. Thus, the myth is most often used to explain the seasons; when Persephone is with Hades, the land is cold and barren, but the land is fertile and fruitful again when she is with her mother.

However, there is far more to it from an energetic perspective than this goddess's story reveals. For one, despite it being her life story, she has little involvement in it at all. She is at the beck and call of the other gods around her. Is Demeter doing what she feels is suitable for her daughter, or what she feels is best for herself, a case of if I can't have her, no one can? Hades clarifies that Persephone changes him for the better, but does he ever consider her feelings? He even resorts to "drugging" her to keep her. And Zeus seems most concerned about appeasing Demeter and the masses than his own daughter. The whole tale appears to disregard the central character, who just goes along with everything, powerless and voiceless, it would seem.

Even though you may feel very powerless at times, childlike or without a voice, you are not. You can be the passenger in your life if that is what you think makes your life easier; sit back and let it happen, but when you take a step back and look at what is happening, you will see that is no life at all. If you are a mother or a carer for others, you may have come across the expression "anything for a quiet life." It is used in relation to people giving in to the demands of others to keep them quiet or make things go away, rather than have the perceived hassle of addressing the actual need. As a mum, I have used the TV as a distraction, given in to sweets, or bought toys to keep my child "happy." But we all know where that can lead to, just pushing greater discomfort further down the line. Not so easy to manage a 6-foot-plus, testosterone-filled young man, or strong-willed young woman, when they start on the "I want" gravy train, especially if it was ingrained from a young age or it worked in the past …

Persephone's influence is exerted most often via feelings rather than a manifestation of her being. Like in the middle of an argument, when you may get a sense of "why bother" and simply give way to the other person for no reason. She may present herself via the easiest of options, whether it is right for you or not. Rather than standing up to nagging or persistent harmful behaviour and demands, you just say "whatever" and let people have their way. Rather than work a little harder at a project to achieve the best possible outcome, you settle for doing far less and just getting by with an average result. Or you find yourself happy to let others make the big decisions in life for you, even the little ones, like when a partner asks where you would like to go out to eat, or which film to see, or where to go for a walk, you just let them decide. You may find soon they stop asking, and you end up doing things you don't want to, being with people who disregard your input, until you find yourself almost invisible in your own life story. Giving your power over to others is not the same as learning from others or asking for and receiving their help, or listening to them when they have something to say.

◎ ACKNOWLEDGING YOUR POWER VISUALISATION

The purpose of this exercise is to feel comfortable in your power and your place in the world. To be powerful is not a bad thing; it is something that we naturally have. Yet, many people spend their lives avoiding this energy within and end up trying to grab power in the outer world. Power comes from the natural expression of your authentic selves—who you really are.

YOU WILL NEED:

* A quiet space where you can be undisturbed for fifteen to twenty minutes

Go to your chosen place in the stillness of the night and make yourself comfortable by either sitting or lying down. Take three deep breaths, in through the nose and out through the mouth. Now close your eyes and breathe steadily, in and out through the nose. Your authentic self is an expression of the powerful lifeforce that exists in every living thing on Earth. Still with your eyes closed, see yourself now as a mighty oak tree, your roots extending deep into the soil, your trunk wide and sturdy, your branches reaching into the skies and teeming with all sorts of life, from insects and birds to small mammals making their homes in and on you. Your power sustains all this life, and in return, your roots draw up nutrients from the earth and your leaves channel water down into your trunk. Allow yourself to be in this space, giving and receiving life, for as long as it feels comfortable.

Gradually come back to your authentic self and let your mind's eye, your inner vision, now float upwards, for you are also the stuff of all the stars in the cosmos. See yourself now in the vast, deep blue void of the cosmos with countless stars all around you. You have no physical body; it is just your essence, your energy, that holds you effortlessly in the quiet, beautiful place where nothing is either good or bad, just pure and perfect as it is, as you are. Allow yourself to be in this vast space of infinite possibilities, of perfect balance between light and dark, for as long as it feels comfortable. Returning to your body to the place you are sitting or lying in, know that all the energy it takes to manifest everything you have seen and been, from a mighty oak to a brilliant white star, exists in you and that you can call upon it anytime.

In our authentic form, we are all divine, and experiencing this through visualisation or meditation helps you get used to that reality. We all wear robes of light that express our unique talents and gifts. Take some time now, in front of your focal point, in the presence of your ancestors, the elements, and directions, to be comfortable with this fact. Sometimes when we experience our authentic self, when we experience our true power for the first time, it can be an overwhelming event, and you may even want to record some of what your divine self senses. If you wish, write them down on paper, fold it neatly, and keep it on your focal point. If you need a reminder of what or who you are in truth at any time, you can read this account.

In looking back at the experiences of Persephone again, at the life that was mapped out for her, where she became the willing pawn in a game of chess between the deities who were more interested in their happiness rather than hers, we can see how quickly you can become a passenger in your own life. To continually depend on others' decision-making, adopt and believe what they believe, and comply with all they say and do without question can be soul-destroying. You may think the easier path is to say "yes" regardless, but it may never become a happier or more fulfilling one. In complete contrast is our next goddess, whose energy is so powerful that she is often called upon to pave the way for something new.

Daring to Destroy

The Hindu goddess of death, time, and doomsday, Kali, is often associated with sexuality and violence. Still, she is also considered a strong mother figure and a symbol of motherly love. Kali is also associated with Lord Shiva, who is her consort. Kali is his power-house, actively provoking and encouraging him. Outside of Asia, she is more often seen as a sinister goddess of death and destruction. In truth, hers is a story of great complexity, and her energy transcends the simplistic narrative of good versus evil. Kali's humble beginnings saw her energy first manifest as one of the seven tongues belonging to Agni, the god of fire. Many hundreds of years later, she evolved into a battlefield goddess in her own right, appearing as the personification of the wrath of Durga as in the epic battle with the demon Raktabija. Things were not going well, as every drop of blood that was spilt by the demon transformed into a deadly fighting clone. Kali, in her guise as Durga's wrath, overwhelmed the demon and all the clones. She drained the demon of his blood before any more could be spilt and then devoured all the clones.

When this fearless, ferocious aspect of her appears to you, it can be both terrifying and intimidating; her blackened skeletal frame is covered in animal skins, and she carries with her a skull-topped staff. This is a game-changing moment; whatever it is in your life that is either hurting you or stopping you from doing what your heart tells you to must come to an end. You need to take charge, even if that means it will impact others or cause discomfort.

My encounter with her was an extraordinary sensory experience. Though at the time I did not see her, for my eyes remained closed, I heard her, approaching across the room, a faint clattering, as she crawled toward my bedside, the jewels on her many arms chiming softly together. I sensed her hands on my arms as she began to dismantle me, piece by piece. It was a most intoxicating experience, and though it felt like every bit of my physical body was being devoured, there was no pain. I could smell fruit, just on the turn, a heady sweetness. In my mind's eye, I could see myself returning to the earth, piece by piece, as Kali picked me apart. Then all was dark. I awoke in the morning, fully intact but with a clear memory of all that went on, and with renewed determination to pursue my purpose.

Kali is primordial: creative, destructive, nurturing, and devouring, but ultimately benevolent. When this aspect of her is called upon, she is referred to as Kali Ma or Divine Mother. Kali's image reflects her complexity. Her protruding red tongue is both a sign of modesty and a thirst for blood. Her eyes are all-seeing. Her full bosom is a sign of nurture and desire. Her unruly black hair hints at unrestrained blood lust and the metaphysical mystery of death that encircles life. And her nakedness is an embodiment of both sensuality and purity.

The way she stands is full of duality; the respectable right-handed path is depicted by her right foot forward stance. In contrast, the transgressive left-handed path is downplayed. Kali's right hands are associated with positive gestures of blessings and forgiveness. In contrast, her left hands hold weaponry, including a bloodied trident, a severed head, and a skull cup. But even these symbols have a greater purpose: the sword symbolising higher knowledge, the head epitomising the ego that must be severed so that the soul can be set free.

Four Acts of Calling in the Destroyer

It is an old teaching that, in order to create something new, something first must be destroyed.

The old form is dismantled till all that remains is its essence, and from this energetic reservoir, something new arises, like a phoenix rising from the ashes. For all human beings, the shedding of skin, for example, allows healthier skin cells to continue the function of this our largest organ. And within women, the lining of the womb perishes and is shed so that the following month the new egg will have a sustainable environment in which to develop. Destruction and death are the catalysts for new beginnings. Thus, understanding the appropriate use of destruction is vital to keep things evolving. In principle, there are four areas of our lives that most of us need to allow some form of release to retain a healthy, energetic balance.

The first area relates to possessions. The more we have, the more we are held captive; the more we are attached to our possessions, the greater our life force is given over to them. Therefore, we hand over control and personal power to these possessions and retain less control and personal power for ourselves. Lakota Native Americans practice a form of "giveaway" in which all they possess is given to the tribe. It is believed that this act will rid the individual of any attachments to what they owned that has the potential to rob them of their personal power and the power they need to reach their spiritual goals. For most people, it is enough to demonstrate that they are willing to give up all that they have to show they are already able to control their sense of attachment and can therefore continue on their path or emotional and spiritual development. The idea of a "spring-clean," based on the old religions of Europe, touches on the same principle.

Next, I would ask you to question your beliefs; are they outdated or a result of indoctrination? Do they still serve you? You see, our beliefs require energy to keep them functioning., and this becomes particularly draining when we hold opposing beliefs simultaneously. This can be paralysing and can stop someone from making choices or take action. Most of our belief systems were chosen for us when we were very young, and it is critical in adulthood to look again at these beliefs to discover what still has meaning and aids us on our path, and what does not help our development.

Another complication is when we identify so closely with our beliefs that we can no longer differentiate between a belief and "me." This then leads to seeing other people who hold differing or opposing views as the enemy because they are against "me" when, in truth, they simply hold a different opinion. Wars have been and continue to be fought over nothing more than a different belief. Please take the opportunity to systematically go through your beliefs and find out how closely identified with them you are. Call on Kali's courage, for you will be surprised at how dearly you hold or how "close" some of your beliefs are to you.

Sitting comfortably, begin by making a list of categories like men, women, work, life, marriage, money, people, friends, health, foreigners, doctors, lawyers, bosses, car salespeople, etc., and then sit with the list and think about one category at a time. Write down on the left side of the paper any beliefs that come forward that no longer fit or serve you now. Then go back, and to the right of each belief you have written, write out the exact opposite belief or a belief that currently serves you. Cut off the left side of the paper and tear it up or burn it for symbolic destruction. Fold up and place the right side of the paper on your focal point.

Next, it is time to look at eliminating habits that no longer serve you. This includes all behaviours that come mechanically and unconsciously, for they keep you unaware of the web of power around you. Habits serve to make life easier and more comfortable for you, but become a problem when we repeat them without thinking and therefore give up an amount of responsibility or choice. You could argue that it is an action heavily influenced by the energy of Persephone when what you need is a touch of Kali's intervention. Looking to work on the appropriate use and management of our emotions, it is always more helpful to come from a place of choice and question the validity of any set ways. If you discover true value in the pattern of behaviour, you can continue with it, but in a more conscious way.

And the fourth area, possibly the most challenging, is relationships. They serve us one way or another, or we won't maintain them; however, we rarely ask ourselves, "What do my relationships really serve?" Look at this from the perspective of your emotional maturity and spiritual growth. Relationships that serve you selfishly seldom serve your development; instead, they tend to reinforce old patterns that keep you stuck and drain you of your personal power. Our thoughts have real power and influence, and the way people hold you in their esteem directly affects your wellbeing.

Malevolent thoughts of ill will are an attack on your power base. Walk away from toxic relationships; it does not help you to maintain relationships that undermine your personal power, just as it is a drain to maintain relationships out of guilt. Be fearless, but not ruthless; don't just run away because it gets hard, or avoid natural emotions that come up during a disagreement. Some testing relationships can serve our highest good.

Calling in this goddess energy can illuminate, separate, and validate all the aspects of your life that you must release, and all the things you should embrace fully. Looking back on my encounter with Kali, it was almost fantastical to believe but equally too intense to ignore. At the time, I didn't even know the power that manifested that day in the room, nor could I conceive why. I simply let it reside in me until the time came to bring it out and make sense of it, which over time is what happened as I researched more about the goddesses, energy work, and our eternal connectedness to the physical, emotional, and spiritual planes. Though you are very much in a physical body, it is influenced by energies from various sources, two of which have real and direct impacts on the goddesses and us.

Out of this World Influencers

As the people and circumstances around you influence you, so are all things on Earth affected by the other cosmic bodies in Earth's orbit and space. Which, in turn, affects us on all levels, emotionally, physically, and for many people, spiritually too. We always have been and always will be energetic manifestations because, as has been said, we are all the stuff of stars. It is much in that same analogy that the energies we associate with goddesses are also influenced and related to cosmic bodies. When looking at Persephone, at the energy that wants to remain compliant, passive, and hold the status quo, there is a direct correlation to our nearest cosmic partner, the moon. And in contrast, when looking at Kali, at the energy that instigates action, aggression, and heralds change, it is the sun to which this energy relates.

I would like you to now imagine that the earth is your cosmic identity, the moon is Persephone's, and the sun is Kali's. For you to thrive, to keep a healthy balance of life and all the elements, all the seasons, all the processes functioning as they should, you need to maintain just the right relationship with both the moon and the sun. Though so much smaller than the sun, the moon exerts a much stronger pull as it is so much closer to us. What happens when you create a situation or relationship and get stuck in it, like a job you no longer enjoy, or a person you no longer love? That situation is like the moon, so close to you, such strong ties; if Persephone's energy overwhelms you, energetically speaking, the temptation to keep things just as they are for an easier life is powerful. What is required is to shine a little sunlight on the situation, just enough to show you what is possible.

But what if your life seems like a neverending car crash, where nothing ever improves despite all the constant changes you make, or discussions you have, or houses you move to, or people you meet, or jobs you find? If, despite all your efforts, there is no satisfaction, and you feel as if you are on the verge of total burnout, then you probably are flying too close to the sun. The sun resides much farther from us than the moon but exerts no less influence because of its mass and power. But this Kali energy is far less predictable and far more volatile than that of Persephone. So engage the sun with even greater care and caution. When it feels like your life is about to crash and burn, then what is required is a little intervention: seek help, and let that help be the driving force in your life for a while.

◎ SUN AND MOON SALUTATIONS EXERCISE

Rebalancing our desire to sit back and let things happen or stand up and make things happen is an ongoing process. Because energy is fluid, you may waver between taking action and letting things slide even during a single day. The process is about understanding how far is "comfortable" or "healthy" for you personally to dwell either in a place of control or in a place of compliance. There will come a time when you feel physically or emotionally exhausted at having to "do" everything and always instigating action. There may also come a time when you are frustrated at feeling disempowered, invisible, or persecuted at the hands of other people or society at large. A way to allow energy, feelings, and actions to flow again is to engage with the celestial bodies that exert the most direct influence on us and our goddess energy.

YOU WILL NEED:

* An elevated space outside, like a small hilltop, roof terrace, or balcony, where you will ideally be able to have a clear view of the sky to the east and west (the best time for this is during the full moon phase once a month at dawn when the sun is awakening on the eastern horizon, while the full moon is on the western horizon and still visible)

* Small handheld bell or rattle for clearing (if desired)

* A small compass if you are not sure of your orientation

Having found your elevated place, energetically "clear" it using your bell or rattle if you so wish. Do this bit, shaking the tool from top to toe, then back up from toe to the top of your head and then in a circle around the area you are standing; arms-length is fine. Whether you have chosen to clear or not, it is essential to set your intention now. In this case, the intention is to connect simultaneously with and acknowledge the sun's and the moon's energies. Now stand facing north (this is where a compass comes in handy) and simultaneously extend your arms out to the side, palms facing upward, and raise them to about shoulder height, or a level comfortable for you. Your right hand is now a conduit for the energy of the sun, and your left hand is now a conduit for the energy of the moon.

Close your eyes and allow yourself to feel these energies, and don't be afraid; the earth you are standing on grounds you. Turn your head to the east, smile, and greet the rising sun, then turn your head to the west, smile, and greet the fading moon. Invite them to release as much or as little of their energy to you as your emotional body requires. You may even notice a shift in energy, like one hand and arm feeling heavier or lighter than the other. This is fine, and again do not worry as the earth grounds you. Just relax your head, either to one side or on your chest and breathe steadily in through the nose and out through the mouth. You are now going to incorporate these two complementary cosmic forces to ensure that you hold the right balance of these energies for the journey you are undertaking at this time in your life.

For the next few minutes, feel the cool gentle moon energy flow through your left hand and arm into your heart centre as the warmer pulsating sun energy flows along your right hand and arm into your heart centre. Gently allow your hands and arms to rest by your side and repeat, either aloud or in your mind, *Gentle moon and spirited sun, I welcome your help with the work I have begun. If I need to do more, to take charge and lead, then spirited sun allow me to retain more of your power to proceed. But if I need to step back, let others lead the way, then please gentle moon allow more of your presence to stay.* Next, imagine you are opening the floodgates of your heart, and excess energies of either the sun or moon flow out, down through your torso and legs, through your feet, into the ground below to be taken up by the earth and recycled. Take a few deep breaths, open your eyes, and go about your day.

Now, it would be pretty naïve to expect that you won't ever have to face either the carnage that Kali can bring or be left in the corner for life to pass you by once you have undertaken the above exercise like Persephone's will might impose. The point is that soon you are able to recognise when either of the emotional and energetic states is out of kilter, causing more harm than good. And even if it does come to an extreme situation, you can recognise this imbalance and be better equipped to restore harmony, and less likely to be entirely overwhelmed by it. You can greet the sun and the moon as often as you wish; you may find the need diminishes greatly as your life becomes less of an energetic or emotional rollercoaster.

Going Along for the Ride

Being taken for a ride in life is very different from going along for a ride. The first implies you have no say in your own life, whereas the second demonstrates you have such mastery of who and where you are in life that you can enjoy watching all you have done, worked hard for, unfold before you just as you desired it to. Going along for the ride from time to time is one of life's real pleasures. But it can only be fully appreciated when you are confident enough to do this—for example, letting someone else choose how to decorate the house or buy a new car without getting caught up in the outcome. It can also mean you are happy to step up and make a few decisions, like changing jobs, picking out where to eat, or deciding what to cook, without worrying about what other people will say about your choices.

You may find you are predominantly drawn to Kali's energy to make the decisions not just for yourself but for others too, especially if they rely on you either at home, at work, or in the community.

It may be a requirement of your purpose to be the leader, take the tough decisions, or motivate others. This is fine too, so long as it doesn't become harmful to you or others. Plenty of people will gravitate to those with the broadest shoulders; you will never be short of willing participants who are more than happy to let you carry their loads. You will need to strike a balance in your life and practice things that enable you to "let go," to relax to trust in the ability of others and the energies all around you. Know that to request help is never a sign of weakness but an expression of the resolve you have to improve your situation or learn more.

If you are drawn to the energy of Persephone, where life appears to happen to you, and you just react to it, it may be a requirement to follow rather than dictate orders, to listen more than you speak. That is also okay, so long as you are aware that others do not always know better, and if you do what they say and things go wrong, you can still be held accountable. Doing only what others say is not the most blameless route through life, and seldom is it painless either. Plenty of people are only too eager to take control; be it financial, physical, or emotional, you will never be short of a willing master who is more than happy to manage your life. You'll need to strike a balance in your life and practice things that enable you to take back control, step into your power, and trust your abilities and the energies around you. Know that to fight for what is right is never a sign of aggression, but an expression of resolve; you have to reclaim your power and improve your situation.

Shut Up or Put Up, Resolution Tips

To enjoy our emotional experience of life to the full, either for moments or for whole years at a time, minimising the opportunities for drastic fluctuations or extreme highs and lows in our lives is all about inviting in the energies of the goddesses that counter what you are going through. This way, not only do you get to understand and appreciate life from another perspective, but your whole emotional state is enriched and harmonised.

> Through circumstance, or your own deeds and actions, you will find yourself either in the driving seat or as a passenger of your own life. Either can easily become the "norm" for you, and you can either become too reliant on others or too controlling. Neither way of life will be fulfilling.

> Support is at hand when you see these paths as extremes of the ideal way and begin to look at ways to readdress the balance. Practising meditation for clarity can help you regain control and responsibility. Using meditation for calm can help you see that giving up excess control and power can help you rebuild relationships and ease stress and tension.

> The goddess Persephone's story is a clear example of how easily you can relinquish your personal power, either to please, to keep the peace, or simply because you don't feel able to speak out for yourself and your

interests. Remember, you are no longer a child nor a slave to others, so take back your voice, direction, power, and sovereignty and create your life again.

Visualisations offer a great window into what can be. By acknowledging your power and your creative force through visualisations, you take the first steps to building your confidence and accepting your responsibilities to yourself, which will also positively impact those around you.

Part of your transformation from the role of the passenger could be to call in the goddess that resides on the other end of the spectrum, Kali. Understanding why and when Kali manifests in our lives, and how we manage that power, that level of control helps us determine how we wisely and respectfully use that energy for the best outcome.

In working with Kali, we seek to review four key areas: our relationship to our possessions, our beliefs, our habits, and our relationship to others. The goddess energy here can help us release what no longer serves via personal but effective actions like a "giveaway."

Looking to the cosmos not only reminds us of our origins, for we are all the stuff of stars, but it also helps us to connect with two of the most prominent tangible "bodies" that affect not only how all

life thrives on Earth but how we thrive as individuals too. The moon and sun move us physically and
emotionally; they sustain us energetically, but again
a predominance of one over the other is ultimately
damaging, so try the salutations exercise to help
release the excesses of these influences and restore
what is lacking.

With a better understanding of where your emotional
strengths and weaknesses lie, and with suggestions
to bring them into greater equilibrium, you can
confidently choose when in your life you wish to
take a back seat and when you need to drive the
whole show, or if you can be comfortable to do a
little of both.

CHAPTER 6

Sitting in Judgement

T urning points come in life when we suddenly see a glimpse of all that lies ahead, of our roles in the world, and the potential consequences of our actions. Mastering this moment means we can employ it effectively, time and time again, in all situations in life, just like the Egyptian goddess Ma'at who you will soon be introduced to. It is about doing the "right" thing, what serves best, not always what we want to do. And a key component is discernment—being able to judge well both the best action and when it is best to take that action. Discernment can be psychological, spiritual, moral, or aesthetic in nature. It involves making nuanced judgements beyond the perception of something. The discerning individual has wisdom and insight, being aware of things that are often overlooked by others.

The ability to discern comes from experiencing life, wrestling with all aspects of it, and the feelings it evokes in us. Over time and if we are willing and open, we begin to pick up these things in other people and situations. Developing this more in-depth understanding can take many years, or happen due to a significant event or trauma. But it is more than just "sensing" something out of the blue; it comes from observation and enquiry, from listening and being attentive. This results in understanding the things that are not right as much as the things that are. Cultivating a discerning mind means being able to digest information and glean that which is worthy or appropriate. And with the access we have to so much information these days, that may mean "kissing quite a few frogs" before you come across what it is worth holding on to.

When I was the editor of a national esoteric publication, my predecessor and owner of the magazine encouraged me to go down into the vaults and read through the backlog of issues. This was suggested not only for me to get an idea of what had already been written about but also to help build up my ability to discern what felt authentic or of interest. This way, I would be more aware of that material when going through the hundreds of submissions that would come in each month. Similarly, when attending a large mind, body, spirit festival, the event founders encouraged me to explore all the different stands and subject matter, and to speak to a wide variety of people. This was not because they thought they would all appeal to me to write about, but again because it would help me judge well what was and what really wasn't of interest. So, in that vein,

I would like to share with you considerations that may help you do the same and give you confidence in your own powers of discernment in whatever situation is important to you.

Exercising Discernment

The ancient Egyptian culture was centred on balance and harmony, with a view that everything had a place and that there was the right place for everything, including within their beliefs, society, and even seasons. What also loomed large in this culture was the unquestionable reverence of their gods and goddesses. And this is where we meet the powerful goddess Ma'at who first and foremost represents the concept of balance and order. In this role, she helped all Egyptians, from pharaoh to pauper, to make sense of the complicated and often inexplicable world around them. Ma'at's energy is said to extend to keeping the stars in motion, allowing the change of seasons to run smoothly. She is instrumental in maintaining heaven and earth's order through her gift of discernment, judging well what to do and when to hold on and what to let go of by upholding truth, justice, balance, and morality.

As a direct descendent of the Egyptian sun deity Ra and partner to the moon god Thoth, the goddess Ma'at held power to decide whether a person would successfully reach the afterlife. The pharaoh Hatshepsut dedicated a small temple to Ma'at at the Karnak temple complex in Luxor. And an earlier Ma'at temple is also indicated in this area by reliefs and stelae belonging to the reign of Amenhotep III. This can be found inside the Precinct of Montu, the smallest of three enclosures at Ipet-Isut. Depictions of Ma'at commonly show a woman either seated or standing with arms outstretched, forming wings. Sometimes she will be holding an ankh, the symbol of life, in one hand and a sceptre in the other.

Another symbol associated with her is an ostrich feather, most commonly depicted as a headdress. The feather alone now symbolises the presence of Ma'at and the feather hieroglyph stands for truth. In the Egyptian Underworld, known as Duat, the hearts of the dead were said to be weighed against the feather of Ma'at. This also explains why, unlike other organs, hearts were left in Egyptian mummies as they were seen as part of the soul. If the heart weighed the same or was lighter than the feather, then it was judged that the deceased had led a "good" life and would go on to Aaru or paradise. A "heavy" heart indicated that the deceased was unworthy, and it was devoured by the goddess Ammit, condemning the dead to remain in the Underworld.

On the mortal plane, it was the chief judge in charge of the Egyptian law courts who embodied the spirit of Ma'at. He served both as a priest and within the judicial system. Court officials wore small golden images of Ma'at as a mark of their authority and fair and balanced judgements. The feather of Ma'at was drawn on the tongues of priests with green dye to ensure that what they spoke was the truth. Rulings would be dealt out according to the nature of the law that had been broken, and the wrongdoings according to the "Principles of Ma'at." Jealousy, dishonesty, gluttony, laziness, injustice, and ungratefulness were all examples of crimes against

Ma'at. Depending on the severity of the crimes and the virtues of the accused, punishments included fines, and corporal or capital punishment.

In the book *Nile Valley Contributions to Civilization*, Tony Browder names the seven principles: truth, justice, harmony, balance, order, reciprocity, and propriety. These principles of Ma'at were the moral rules and beliefs that guided the behaviour of all the people of this ancient society. They helped people understand what was right and wrong, so they profoundly influenced people's actions. These teachings spread to other peoples and cultures, including the Greeks, where Socrates, Plato, and Aristotle reinterpreted them. Principles are seldom spoken about today; in essence, they are any moral rule or belief you uphold that helps you know what is right and wrong, and that influences your actions—in other words, your fundamental truth, core value, or idea that forms the foundations of who you are and how you live. Looking at the principles of Ma'at, you might want to consider our own discernment today. I invite you now to explore them as I have been shown them from the perspective of our goddess energy within:

> Truth is about the definition of reality, the ability to understand the difference between what is real and what is not. When working with goddess energy and your own divinity, the reality is that creative energy is the driving force giving rise to all that exists. So one truth is that you are a creative being and every experience you encounter is a result of that.

Justice is the state in which we all have equal opportunity for our basic needs to be met (food, water, shelter, medical care, safety, dignity, respect, and so on), to live in peace, to meaningfully participate and contribute to society, to offer your essence or talents to the greater good of the whole.

Harmony is the state of being in which the different expressions of spirit or creative energy—people, animals, plants, etc.—exist and evolve in ways that create real beauty and alignment. Be authentic, because that is the only way harmony can genuinely be achieved, and it occurs naturally when you are true to yourself—to your spiritual or creative reality.

Balance is a state in which an individual's internal and external environments are aligned with their creative essence, with each other, and with all creation. It is the experience of holding that place where new possibilities come into being, where opposites meet, and where new life is manifested.

Order is about things occupying the space and place for which they were created, and arranged in ways that are clear, uncluttered, and free of excess.

Reciprocity is all about experiencing the ebb and flow of your actions and life itself, embracing the rhythm of cause and effect, give and take, investment and return that underpins every aspect of creation.

Propriety means to behave and do what is appropriate according to the truth that all humans are creative beings. It means that you seek to express yourself through behaviours, words, actions, thoughts, and feelings without intentionally harming another living thing, including yourself.

The principles might seem "grand" and overwhelming if you tried to live by each one to the letter. But look again, and you will see they are actually based very much on our innate feelings and emotions, on things we instinctively know to be the way to approach the way we go about living our lives. The key is to find, recognise, and listen to your inner voice when making decisions in life, judging a situation, or making choices. Our lives have become complicated because of all the things we have created to add to it, both the material things and our own expectations of what it takes to be content, happy, and to live a good life.

Advances in technology not only give us greater access to each other and information that moulds our view of ourselves and the world, but it also opens us up to the desires and opinions of others. We become a currency for others to trade; we open ourselves to falsehoods, and perpetuate fear and inadequacy. And so the ability to discern, to judge well, in life is now more critical than ever before. The following ritual is a tangible way to help you come to terms with what really matters to you right now, what needs releasing, and what needs attention to move forward. You may only do it a few times in life, or you might find it becomes a good habit to adopt more regularly.

◎ PILLAR OF DISCERNMENT RITUAL

YOU WILL NEED:

* A quiet space indoors where you can be undisturbed for thirty to sixty minutes

* A small handheld bell to "clear" or cleanse the space

* A vessel to contain a piece of burning paper and something to ignite the paper

* Representations of the five pillars' elements; an object made of stone, an object of wood, an object of crystal, an object made of straw, and a feather—any type of feather so long as it is ethically sourced

* Pen and four sheets of paper

Once you have gathered together all you need, go to your chosen space and "clear" it using the bell, ringing it in front of you, behind you, and to either side of you. Then, sit down comfortably on the floor with your pen and paper. Designate one sheet of paper to each of the first four pillar elements by writing "stone," "wood," "crystal," and "straw" across the top.

Next, arrange the representations in a pillar (straight vertical line), in front of you, within easy reach, starting with "stone" nearest to you, then above that "wood," then above that "glass," then above that "straw," and finally, farthest from you at the top, the feather.

Starting with stone

Focus first on the representation of stone closest to you. Pick it up and hold it in your dominant hand. This is the foundation element: so65lid, cold, weighty of substance. Stone holds wisdom and energy of old, your past experiences, as well as unreleased potential. It represents the principles or the standards in your life that are constant, upon which most of what you say and do in life is built. I want you to close your eyes and now think about what really matters to you. Allow whatever wants to come to the fore to do so. It could be raising your children, your health, your partner, happiness, making money or financial security, your work, the environment, saving the world, or saving yourself. It may be even simpler, like cultivating patience, kindness, inner strength, or having your say. Put "stone" back down in the spot closest to you at the base of the pillar, and take the sheet headed "stone" and list these thoughts.

As you allow these thoughts to come about and write them down, notice how each makes you feel. Be aware of where you hold tension or uncertainty around the idea in your body, then perhaps it is not as fundamental to you as you believed. By "judging well" each of the core principles held in stone, you will come to realise what matters to you, what defines you that you are not prepared to relinquish or change, and why. You can then start coming to terms with that and decide whether you let things rest there, or work on them, or indeed release them up the pillar into the wood. You can do this by saying, *By the power of Ma'at in me, I release what no longer resides in stone to be free. I pass it up to the more pliable wood to find a home there or be resolved for my greater good.* Put a line through that thought on the paper and write it again on the paper headed "wood."

Working with wood

Next, focus on the "wood" representation. Pick it up and hold it in your dominant hand. This is the construction element: sturdy, warm, of substance yet pliable. Wood operates with wisdom and energy of both your past experiences and what is new to you, and looks to mould and manifest your potential and desires. It represents the principles or the standards in your life that are important, especially in the present moment, dealing with the day-to-day responsibilities and challenges to keep things evolving and progressing. So close your eyes and now think about the principles or standards you employ daily. It could be your routines, chores, the food you buy and consume, your home, the clothes your wear, how you project to the outside world and what you see for yourself, your hobbies or interests. Put "wood" back down in its place in the pillar, take the sheet headed "wood" and list these thoughts down.

Allow these thoughts to come and write them down; notice how each makes you feel. Where you hold tension or uncertainty around the idea, it is unclear how this works for you. By "judging well" each of the core principles contained in wood, you will realise what works well, what needs to be explored, what you are not prepared to relinquish or change, and why. You can then start coming to terms with that and decide whether you let things rest there, make them part of your foundations, return them to "stone," or gain greater clarity by releasing them up the pillar into "crystal." You can do this by saying, *By the power of Ma'at within, I allow the process of discernment to begin. I pass it up to crystal's scrutiny, to rest a while there, and its purpose becomes clear to me.* Put a line through that thought on the paper and write it again on the paper headed "crystal." Anything that has now established itself as a core principle gets a line drawn through it in "wood" and is added to "crystal."

Calling in crystal

Next, pick it up and hold the crystal representation in your dominant hand. This is the transformation element: engaging, enlightening, of substance yet delicate. Crystal is the conduit of energy; it can amplify, contain, or reduce the attention you invest in your actions. It represents the principles or the standards in your life that are perhaps a little unclear; they may have been inherited or imposed on you, and you need to ask yourself now whether they are authentic to you. So close your eyes and now think about them, where they came from, why you hold on to them, or how you can incorporate them into your way of thinking and living. These ideas may be around your spiritual beliefs, political persuasion, outlook on childrearing, or what you eat and why. Remember to look at what you have written on the crystal paper carried over from "stone" or "wood." Put "crystal" back down in its place in the pillar, take the sheet headed "crystal" and list your thoughts.

As you allow these thoughts to come about and write them down, notice how each makes you feel. Where do you hold tension or uncertainty around the idea? Perhaps it is now clear why this isn't working for you. By "judging well" each of the core principles held in crystal, you will understand what needs to be explored and what you are not prepared to relinquish or change and why. You can then start coming to terms with that and decide whether you need to keep looking into it here, or make it part of your more pliable ideas and return it to wood, or judge it to be no longer of service to you and release up the pillar into "straw." You can do this by saying, *By the power of Ma'at in me, unveil what is shrouded, let the truth be set free. I send to wood what helps to serve my foundation and release to straw what no longer serves as motivation.* Put a line through the thought on the "crystal" paper and write it again on the paper headed "straw." Anything that is now more clearly of value to you gets a line drawn through it in on the "crystal" paper and is added to the "straw paper."

Selecting straw

Turn to your representation of "straw." Pick it up and hold it carefully in your dominant hand. This is the element of release: fragile, easily manipulated, volatile. Straw is the liberator of energy; it sets it free, releases it in its purest, most neutral form back to its source. Straw will make room for new ideas and values to be allowed to come in, and it will help highlight other ideas that can be solidified as core principles. It represents the principles or the standards in your life that no longer serve you and now need to be transformed and released. So close your eyes and now think about the principles, desires, and plans that no longer serve you or are not authentic. You may already have one or two written on the straw paper. It could involve people, job, religion, politics, others behaviour to you. Put "straw" back down in its place in the pillar, take the sheet headed "straw," and list these thoughts down.

As you allow these thoughts to come about and write them down, notice how each makes you feel. Where you hold tension or uncertainty around the idea, then perhaps it is unclear where you are ready to let go. By "judging well" each of the ideas held in straw, you will know what must be released or what perhaps still resonates with you a little. You can do this by saying, *By the power of Ma'at in me, release what no longer serves, what I must set free. I send to crystal what may still be of worth and release all that remains to the sky and the earth.* Put a line through those things you need to look at further on the "straw" paper and write it again on the paper headed "crystal." And take a good look at what remains on the straw paper. You will release these thoughts, ideas, beliefs, and principles for the greater good, permanently.

Finishing with feather

Finally, we come to the "feather" representation. This is your feather of Ma'at, the tool for casting the released principles' energy out to be put to better use elsewhere, in another time and another place. Take your vessel for burning paper and then take the sheet of paper headed "straw." Either scrunch up or tear up the sheet so you can safely burn it, place it in the vessel, and ignite it with care. Allow the paper to burn up safely, then take your feather and wave it carefully over the burnt remains and say, *By the power of Ma'at in me, release what no longer serves, set it free. I send to the source, via the ether all around, energy purified when it is found. May it serve a greater purpose honest and plain and allow what I need now to expand and remain.* Put the feather back in its place and tidy up your space, being sure to clean out your vessel for burning. You can keep the remaining three sheets with your principles on your focal point or somewhere safe that you can return to as and when necessary. Should you wish to do this ritual again, you will have a record of your "principles" from this first ritual to work with or serve as a reminder.

This ritual serves not only to examine your own principles, but also to examine the actions and motivations of what drives you in a very tangible and organised manner. The ritual itself is an exercise in practising some of Ma'at's fundamental principles like "truth," "harmony," "order," and "propriety." Soon you will be more aware of how the things you say and do are in line with your principles or not. And rather than being over critical with yourself or overly judgemental, you will be able to deal with these thoughts and ideas more constructively—moving them up or down your "pillar."

When the Heart Weighs Heavy

Suppose you were to look for Ma'at in literature, search for her online, or watch documentaries. You will see her tied in with the image of the weighing up of a heart and a feather, and it is often linked to the expression "a heavy heart." She is shown as being youthful in appearance, with generic features that were considered beautiful for that time, and dressed in a manner appropriate to her power and status. All this is relatively standard practice for depicting a deity, which is more about energetic presence than a physical one.

Ma'at's energy expresses itself by way of the hundreds of decisions we make every day. Most are made on autopilot, like getting dressed, what to eat for breakfast, the route to work or to the shops, and so on. In this "space," you are very unlikely to actually "see" Ma'at; she generally saves that for more significant and usually more heart-wrenching decision-making times in our lives. Does this mean that when the time comes, she will appear before you, extract your heart, and measure it against the weight of her ostrich feather? Probably not. When the time comes, you are far more likely to feel the weight of the decision you must make in your heart and the consequences pulling at your heartstrings.

Whether you find yourself in the position to "pass judgement" (i.e., you are making the decisions that impact others) or finding yourself "being judged" where the decision-making is out of your hands, you can find yourself dealing with difficult emotions. In the myth of Ma'at, it is the heart that is impacted by everything you say and do in your life, so the more negativity, trauma, wrongdoings, etc., the heavier your heart. Imagine then a whole lifetime of expending energy on containing what no longer serves you; what you did wrong, what pain was inflicted on you, and what trauma you might have caused others; all of it taking up residence either permanently or for a while at least, in the one place that keeps your body alive. You will recognise this feeling; though your heart is actually no heavier, it will feel like it is struggling under the pressure of the decisions being made.

Understanding why this has happened goes a long way to relieving some of that pressure, even if it pains you. You may not get the answers by merely asking the questions, and if it involves another person, they may also not be willing to explain, so this is when you need a clear head for your heavy heart. And this is when you can also draw on the energy of Ma'at, the energy that allows you to see both sides, even if the reason for an action is not apparent; being able to accept that alone can make a huge difference. Just as with the balancing act that Ma'at performs, there must be two sides to everything, and sometimes that is all you will have to go on. Accept it and move on.

Equally, when asking for answers when a decision made has gone against you, there may be a plethora of reasons. This can be just as hard to take as no answers at all; most people would go on the defence when faced with that, but you can turn that around. Listen to each reason and be honest with yourself when exploring if that is true or not. Though you will seldom be able to change a person's mind by arguing back at this stage, you might just learn a thing or two and be able to move forward. Again, this is another way of transforming the energy into something constructive and relieving a little more pressure from your heart. This might sound flippant, but the intention is to use creative power to transform situations that help us cope with whatever comes our way.

You might have to make decisions that others disagree with or find baffling, leaving them reeling and wanting answers. This, too, can weigh heavily on your heart. Therefore, be clear about why you have decided this, think it through, and be as honest as you can be. Being honest without spite, venom, anger, or blame helps a great deal, though it may not always be possible. But the more we practice honesty and transparency in our decision making, the easier it becomes, and the better the outcomes will be. Again, remember you are powerful. The energy you use to manifest your words and deeds is neutral and can go either way, so choose to use it in a constructive rather than destructive way when making decisions and giving the reasons for those decisions.

Looking at the principle of balance—key to this chapter, key to making the right choices for the best outcome, and vital to living a fulfilling and enjoyable life—we now look at the tools that Ma'at uses to balance her scales of judgement, namely the heart (the way in which a person lived their life, their conduct, their struggles, and their triumphs) and the feather (representing their spirit, the purest existence possible for that person). You would be forgiven for thinking there will never be a time when the heart will be as light as a feather, so it is an impossible expectation. But not so; speaking energetically and practically, it is all about how you deal with life that matters, not that your life is lived in a pristine, faultless manner; you would not be here on earth if that were the case, for we are having a human experience.

◎ Honouring the Heart Meditation

Part of that experience is to make mistakes, to get things wrong, to behave and even judge in such a manner that we can cause harm. What we do about all of those things is what Ma'at looks at when weighing us up. Do you learn from your mistakes? Do you admit when you get things wrong and take responsibility for your actions? Do you recognise when you cause harm and work to find ways to manage those actions better? Are you looking after your "heart" energetically, and are you using your feather "energetically" so that you can make better choices along your own path of creativity? I invite you now to look at these incredible tools, honour and appreciate them, and put them to use, enhancing your experience of this life you have from a place of greater harmony and self-awareness.

YOU WILL NEED:

* A quiet space where you can be undisturbed for ten to fifteen minutes

Lie on your back and gently wiggle your fingers and toes to release tension. Whilst lying still, take three deep breaths, in through the nose and out through the mouth. Allow your body to relax and sink into the floor. Take one deliberate deep breath in, allowing your chest to expand, and on the out-breath, push the collar bones wider apart, really opening up the area that holds the heart. Continue to breathe steadily. Now close your eyes and bring one hand to your heart and the other to rest on the top of your belly. Giving your attention to the space beneath and between your hands, your chest and abdomen, notice it rise and expand on the in-breath and fall and contract as you breathe out, creating space for new awareness.

Now on the next in-breath, imagine you are drawing in emerald light. It comes in through your nose and makes its way to your heart, flooding that space with warm healing energy; hold the breath. As you breathe out, allow the emerald-green light to expand throughout your entire torso. Take a few more breaths like this, in through the nose, filling your heart centre, expanding into your torso, then gently out through the mouth. By opening your heart centre this way, you allow the things that weigh heavy there to be lifted and released and fill the void those feelings and emotions leave with love and compassion for yourself and others that can then be extended outwards into your everyday decision-making process.

Next, call to mind a person or several people whom you love. See their faces with your mind's eye and now allow the emerald-green light you have swirling inside you to extend out to them. Continue to breathe steadily. Next, visualise before you a situation or relationship that is causing you concern; perhaps it is one-sided or too confrontational. See the face of the person involved and again allow the emerald-green light to extend to them. Breathe steadily as you allow more of the emerald-green healing light to envelop that situation. You are not looking for any answers or any resolution at this stage; you are just seeking to feed that situation or relationship with healing light. Now picture yourself, lying here in the room, and see your face looking back at you. And now allow all the love and compassion the emerald-green healing light carries to envelop the face before you. As your heart opens, allow as much time as you need to flood yourself, the image of you in your mind's eye, with pure, healing energy.

Now, when you are ready, gradually come back to your authentic self and let any visions before you now fade, and the green healing light returns to your heart space. Allow your breathing to return to normal and rest your hands by your side on the floor. Know that all the healing energy you will ever need to lighten the load on your heart can be accessed at any time and that the source is limitless. Again, when you feel ready, open your eyes, wiggle your fingers and toes, stand up, and go about your day. The meditation you have just done is one way of honouring your heart and allowing it to do what it needs to function well emotionally with the bonus of helping the heart physically, too, by combating emotional stress.

But as we have seen, the heart is just one part of Ma'at tools of discernment, the other being the feather, and so it would be remiss of me not to help you with that part too. What follows is practical information and guidance about featherwork in spiritual practices that also aid us when it comes to working with goddess energy and our creative force.

Your Feather of Ma'at

When working with creative energy and all the earthly elements, there is a good chance that you will use tools that consist of animal parts. Feathers are a prime example, and with all such generous gifts from Mother Nature, it is important to know how to respectfully and honourably acquire them, prepare them for use, and care for them. I remember once driving a highly respected "wise-woman" to an important meeting out in the countryside. About thirty minutes into the journey, it became evident we were heading in totally the wrong direction. But for me to do a U-turn, I had to drive a little farther along the road and, just at the point where I could turn around, my passenger noticed a dead crow in the road. Immediately we stopped so she could collect it to give it a proper burial and utilise the wings later. Once she had the bird safely wrapped up in a bag, she turned to me and said with a smile, "See, we were meant to come down this road." And with that, I turned the car around, and we headed off to our destination. It's good to know what to do because you never know with feathers when they will offer their blessing.

If you're preparing a feather of an animal found dead (or one that dies in front of you), you will need to ensure that it is free of insects, like maggots. Avoid using any feathers from a dead animal that smells; the risk of disease is too high. Bear in mind that unless you witnessed the bird perish in front of you, there is still a risk from something it might have carried, like a disease. The key to preserving any feather, either taken directly from a dead bird or found on its own, is to remove all moisture.

So take a plastic bag large enough to hold the feather without bending the ends and fill it halfway with salt (table salt is acceptable). Put the feather into the bag and fill it with salt, so the feather is completely encased. Seal the bag and leave it for a few days. From a creative or spiritual perspective, the salt (as a representation of the earth) will begin to transform the energies that no longer serve the wing for its future use. After a few days, remove the feather and check that it is completely dry. You're now free to clean it and prepare it for use as a tool.

To ensure your feather is free of mites and to "future proof" it against such parasites, lay it on and cover it with rosemary, lavender, or tea tree for a day or two. You can then coat the feather with a fine spray of either vodka or rose water. I read once that "alcohol expands the spiritual nature of a tool but doesn't expand the soul structure," so be sure not to do it too often to distort the tool's power. Now the feather is ready to be put to use for smudging, with other feathers in a fan, or for your pillar ritual, for example.

Be sure to store your feather where it is out of harm's way (moisture or mites, etc.). Keeping it in a cedarwood box, for example, will do the trick, and it can be placed on your focal point. It is also important to be aware that not all feathers are fair game, even if you just found them on the ground. Check out any restrictions; for example, the Migratory Bird Treaty Act of the USA makes it illegal to own feathers from many native birds. Please do respect these laws as they are for the protection of the animals and allow us to utilise only what we need with honour and integrity. As this is part of your experience with Ma'at, be discerning and judge well!

Making the difficult choices in life need not throw you into turmoil and cause your heart to despair, because often the difficult decisions, when taken with discernment, have the best outcomes for all involved. Remember to listen to your intuitive voice when meeting people and "passing judgement" on them. When in those first few moments you ask yourself, will they be good for me? Do I have some common ground with them? Do I find them attractive? There will be some obvious answers forthcoming, but exercising discernment is also about timing, having the patience to allow some things to unfold with time, to make sure you have enough information before deciding one way or another.

When it comes to relationships and people, not everything is revealed straight away, and passing judgement too soon may close doors on potential friendships and even love. Regret can weigh very heavy on the heart. Like the weighing up Ma'at undertakes of feather and heart, of the essence of a person and their deeds, be sure you have the measure of the scales right in the first place!

Sitting in Judgement, Resolution Tips

In life, try as you might, you cannot avoid making tough decisions from time to time. And to weigh up the reasons for and against something, whether to stay or go, whether to find a way to make things better or find a way to thrive with the way things are, are all so much easier to do when you are open and honest with yourself and transparent with others. Knowing you have done what is necessary to get to this point of "judging well" should fill you with a certain amount of confidence and enable you to move forward with conviction. Being accepting when you are at the receiving end of someone else's decisions can be made less traumatic when you remove yourself from the victim's role in all of it and instead employ coping strategies to move on. You won't always have the answer, but you will be okay with that fact and moving forward is a most liberating quality. All of these things can be practised and cultivated, so I ask you to bear in mind ...

> Discernment—being able to judge well both the best action and when it is best to take that action can be psychological, spiritual, moral, or aesthetic. It comes from experiencing life at a deeper level, which may take years to master or happen suddenly due to a significant event.
>
> There are ways to fine-tune your ability to discern. These include: considering the source of your information (not everything is always accurate, nor can everything be found on the internet, for example); seeking the ideas and suggestions of others, whether they agree and support what you believe or not; and allowing for the challenging or unexpected, which is especially true of relationship dynamics.
>
> Consider the principles upon which your decision and choices are based. The principles of Ma'at can serve as helpful guidelines even in today's world, based on the following considerations: truth, justice, harmony, balance, order, reciprocity, and propriety.

Ritual work can help make sense of our thoughts, responsibilities, and priorities and engage us in a physical activity that requires attention and care. Practice the Pillar of Discernment Ritual as often as you need to help you regulate your own principles and connect with various elements.

The goddess Ma'at is the embodiment of our ability to navigate our world through the choices we make. These may be the little day-to-day undertakings or the more significant life decisions that can affect our happiness and others around us.

Ma'at is often depicted as a generic-looking goddess of her time and place. Yet, today she is more likely to manifest as a powerful feeling within our hearts that can be cultivated to bring about greater balance and harmony in our lives.

Sunken, broken, or heavy hearts feel very real to anyone who has suffered emotional turmoil, and they struggle to see the positives in life. But our hearts and our spirits can be lifted and liberated when we understand how to release those feelings, or better still, when we consider the hearts of others more often.

Honouring the heart through meditation is a way of elevating the emotion that gets you down, right where it hits hardest. And it has physical benefits too that affect your whole body.

Featherwork must be undertaken with respect and diligence. Feathers can be used for smudging, as a representation of air on a focal point, as adornment, for ceremonial work, as the embodiment of Spirit or the spirit of an animal, even as the sign of having lived a principled life.

CHAPTER 7
Becoming the Fortress

As a creative being, you will manifest, collect, and attract people, things, and ideas worth keeping precious, safe, and secure. There is much to value and protect in life, and times will present themselves when you need to stand by who you are, especially when you have worked so diligently to discover this. The energy and influence of one particular Greek Titan goddess, Hekate, now holds this ground fearlessly. Discover what the "triple goddess" aspect means to us today and how we can better utilise these aspects to enlighten and guard against anything that intends to harm or instill fear and secure what about us we hold dear.

Becoming a fortress is not about locking yourself up in an emotionally impenetrable tower; it is about having the knowledge, the voice, and the practical tools to defend your authentic self. Psychiatrist Carl Jung said that "the privilege of a lifetime is to become who you truly are."[3] Don't spend your life trying to please others, and society at large, at the expense of being true to yourself, finding happiness, or realising your potential. Remember, you are not defined by your occupation or by the influence of others. Not taking to heart what others think about you may make you stand out from the crowd, but it is an authentic stance.

Cultivating the ability to be true to yourself via your thoughts, words, and deeds is like practically building yourself up, brick by brick. It may require sacrifices, giving up on distractions. For example, if you are in a relationship or a job that makes you miserable and depressed or forces you to act or behave differently from who you truly are, you need to remove yourself from it. Remove yourself from that situation and stand firm in who you really are, surrounded only by what helps rather than hinders.

◎ CIRCLE OF PROTECTION

To stand this strong takes determination, and without having a "virtual fortress" around our authentic self, we can leave ourselves open to all manner of emotional and energetic invasion. Creating healthy habits to protect against such intrusions is useful, especially when building your fortress. The following exercise engages your inner goddess energy, with the natural elements of the four directions and universal energy to give you strength and protection. This will enable you to start working

---

3   Carl G. Jung, *Memories, Dreams, Reflections*, ed. by Aniela Jaffé, trans. Richard Winston and Clara Winston (New York: Vintage Books, 1989).

on your foundations, and give you the courage to build on them as you see fit.

YOU WILL NEED:

* A quiet space, large enough to create a circle of at least five feet in diameter on the floor, where you will be undisturbed for fifteen to twenty minutes
* A white centre candle and something to light it with that can be kept in a pocket
* A small handheld bell for clearing
* A few drops of either lavender or tea tree oil
* An object that represents your inner power, e.g., something from your focal point, or a goddess statue, or a piece of jewellery that empowers you when you wear it. Enough table salt to create a thin rim of a circle, at least four to five feet in diameter

Begin by preparing the space; do this by clearing the area in which you will work. Take your bell and, while ringing it, carefully walk around your space, crisscrossing through the middle of it. Last but not least, ring the bell about your personality too. Now place the bell down in a corner of your space. Then take the white candle, the oil, and your power object to the centre of your space. When placing these objects down, the candle goes in the middle, the power object is placed to the right of the candle, and the oil is set to the left of the candle. Now take your salt and stand in the middle of the space; being sure not to knock over the objects you have just placed there, carefully pour out the salt in a circular rim around you and the items, at least five feet in diameter. (I find that this works best for me by merely holding the salt out at arm's length and releasing it as I slowly spin around in a full circle.) To complete this circle's preparation, we call in the four directions (addressing the east, south, west and north).

Start by facing east, the direction of illumination, of gaining new levels of understanding, and say, *Hail and welcome the energy of the east, protect all that I hold dear by shining your light on the things unseen, and thus remove any fear.* Turn now to the south, the direction of vigour and fulfilment, and say, *Hail and welcome the energy of the south, protect all I hold true by giving me the strength to face the things that I must do.* Turn again to face the west, the direction of contemplation and spiritual realisation and say, *Hail and welcome energy of the west, protect all that is now me by keeping alive my connection to nature's great mystery.* Turn for the last time to face north, the direction of wisdom and survival (physical and emotional) and say, *Hail and welcome the energy of the north, protect all who have gone before, by taking what no longer serves and showing it the door.*

Looking back down to the centre of your circle, it is time to light the candle, then stand up and declare, either aloud or in your head, that only positive, productive, and progressive energy is allowed in your aura. Demand that all other energy leave you now and return to Source. Visualise the room filling with a colour that you associate most with feeling protected and safe. Now put a couple of drops of oil on your dominant thumb and anoint yourself. Start by touching the top of your head, then the centre of your forehead, down to your throat, your heart, the base of your spine, the back of your knees and the bottoms of your feet. Say a prayer of thanksgiving to release the directions, something like, *Sacred Source from which all directions gain their divine energies, thank you for holding me in your protection as I seek to bring wholeness to my heart and all I touch. I release the energy of the directions, in gratitude, with thanks and reverence.*

Now you can extinguish the candle and clear up your space. (A tip here about using salt: though it is not recommended to reuse salt for multiple exercises or rituals, I would always recommend scattering it in the woods, a field, or into the sea or natural flowing water. Allow nature to recycle it naturally.)

You can undertake this exercise as often as you feel necessary, though I would limit it to no more than once a week; otherwise, you will really get through a lot of oil unnecessarily. But remember, you can visualise yourself standing in the middle of the circle with your energy field surrounded and filled with your protective light at any time.

Standing Your Ground

In the early third century BCE, the Athenian Zeno founded "Stoicism," a school of Hellenistic philosophy. The core principle maintains that our path to wellbeing is found by standing firmly "in the moment" and experiencing it without succumbing to the desire for instant gratification or being paralysed by the fear of pain. The practice of remaining attentive in the moment is similar to mindfulness and some forms of Buddhist meditation. It is a reminder of how to be strong, steadfast, and in control of yourself, especially in challenging times. Stoicism's philosophy has much to share with us even today, as it is less concerned with complicated world theories but instead driven by the benefits of practical action. So I invite you to consider the following tips that will help you get into the right state of mind to give you solid footing in life. *Be prepared.* So often, we are encouraged to visualise the positive, the fairytale ending, but by considering the worst-case scenario, what could happen or what you could lose, it helps you prepare for life's inevitable setbacks. Regulating your expectations can protect your soul from disappointments. A contemporary approach is summed up in the expression "Hope for the best, but plan for the worst."

> *Practice self-control.* Learn to distinguish between the things you can control, like your opinions, desires, and actions, and the things beyond your control, like other people, your reputation, and others' actions. It is all about reinforcing the things within your

control and spending your energy there. The key is to practice.

Practice self-care. Other people's opinions are beyond your control, so don't invest your energy in them. But we are social beings, and the fear of being socially ostracised is so deeply ingrained in us that it is much easier said than done. The key is to develop and appreciate your talents and all the positives about yourself; that is what you should care about. How you think and feel about yourself will have the most profound impact on your life experience, so take care of that above all else.

See the bigger picture. Consider how vast the cosmos is: all the life, the energy, the potential, and the amazing things that are manifested. This is a bit like looking at your "tapestry" but on an even bigger scale. It makes you realise how unimportant the trivial things in life are: the overbearing relative, the person who cut you off in traffic, the work colleague with the irritating laugh. Stoic practitioner and emperor Marcus Aurelius explained, "Whenever you want to talk about people, it's best to take a bird's-eye view and see everything all at once."[4] To find the perspective, you need to rise above all the "chatter," look

4   Marcus Aurelius, *Meditations*, trans. Martin Hammond (New York: Penguin, 2006), 89.

down on the earth as the stars do, and develop an altered state of consciousness.

Embrace the moment. This is a mindset, a conscious effort to make the most of whatever happens. Treat each moment as something to embrace, not avoid. Making plans, setting goals, being ambitious are all commendable so long as you remain detached from the outcome. Instead, do your best, and see where it takes you. By going with the flow, following the natural course of things, you will more likely find yourself in a place in line with your nature.

Life is precious. Your time, journey, and experience of this life are limited, and time is ticking. You don't want to waste this time feeding unhealthy emotions or focusing on trivial matters. Reflecting on the fact that we will die at some point (unknown to us) puts your life in perspective. Considering death should not be something that instils fear but instead fills you with a sense of gratitude for life, for the experience that has been gifted to us.

Keep a journal. Writing down your day's events, observations, thoughts, and feelings has a cathartic effect on the soul. You can make your entries as detailed as you wish. By reflecting on the day that has passed, it is a reminder of things you have learned and appreciated, as well as your thoughts, manifestations, and the things that frustrate or upset you. Instead of merely listing the events that happened throughout your day, try to write down thoughts you had or lessons you learned.

As you learn to reflect and meditate on the Stoic doctrines, you learn to retreat into yourself, and slowly you begin to build this inner citadel—a citadel that, even if under siege, can withstand any attack. One which will never fall to anger, greed, lust, desire, fear, pain, delusion, or any other harmful emotion. Retreating into yourself, either in moments of calm or turbulence, to rehearse your maxims, remember death, love your fate, or prepare for what may come your way is profoundly therapeutic. It is to be your own counsel. Retreating into your mind can give you more safety, comfort, and clarity than any citadel made of stone or brick. It will take time to build and will require a lot of patience but persevere. "Your ruling centre is invincible when it retreats into itself and is content in it."[5]

Adopting any one of the above practices can go a long way to positively impacting your emotional well-being and giving you the confidence to stand firm in what you know to be right for you. You do not need to become a "stoic" to benefit from the philosophy if it resonates with you. This way of looking at our place in the world, at how we can become less caught up in the drama or trivia of those things that really shouldn't matter or consume our energy,

5   Aurelius, *Meditations*, 80.

frees us up to put our attention into the parts of us that deserve or need it, into the people we hold dear, and into the actions we need to take to thrive. We thrive by standing up for what we believe in, by shining a light on those things that need to be seen, by unlocking all our potential and helping others to do the same. The goddess that embodies all these things, through all stages of life, whether you experience them as the "maiden," the "mother" or the "crone," now comes forth to give you the strength and confidence to live fearlessly.

She Who Protects

To tell the story of Hekate and her powers, it is probably done best when we put it in a contemporary context. Hekate was effectively thrust into this world as an orphan, for neither of her parents were of this world. So here she is, a very gifted young person, alone in the world. She quickly discovers that this is a world quite hostile towards her gifts. Going about the town, she notices people's daily struggles, their dependence on material things rather than turning to each other, their quest for more to own rather than a search for more knowledge. Children's innocence is stripped away too soon, whilst the wisdom and vulnerabilities of the elderly are ignored too easily. Nature and all living things are consumed without respect or any foresight to give back. A young Hekate is bewildered and perplexed.

Despite all she sees, Hekate does all she can for those around her, but as she grows and develops, so too do her gifts, and it is her gifts that now bring suspicion upon her. She is accused of being evil, unnatural, and dangerous, and she is cast out of her home and town, so she wanders, day and night, with only animals for company and comfort. During the day, she learns the path of the sun and the properties of all the plant life about her. She meets and speaks to strangers and learns of their needs, their ways, and where they come from. She visits many different places. At night she can rest easy in the comforting light of the moon and she gains the trust and understanding of all the creatures of the night, befriending many of them.

Having all this knowledge, she is able to sustain herself during this time, and over the next few years, she begins to hatch a plan. Her keys, torches, and closest companions—two wolves—are all Hekate now needs to become who she was born to be: the wisdom keeper, the way-shower, and the protector. She builds her great fortress and vows to defend the defenceless, light a way for those in darkness, and pass on knowledge to those willing to learn. All others had better watch out because this is one goddess you don't want to get on the wrong side of.

It is widely accepted that the Greeks probably adopted and adapted Hekate from the Thracian people from southern and eastern Europe who worshipped her as "Bendis," their own all-encompassing and all-powerful "Mother goddess." Hekate first appeared in literature in the eighth century BCE, in Hesiod's *Theogony*, as a goddess of great honour with equal dominion over the sky, earth, and sea. Her importance to Byzantium's ancient Greek city (later to become Constantinople and now Istanbul) was first and foremost as a deity of protection. Legend has it that when Philip of Macedon was about to attack the city, Hekate alerted its people with her torches and the warning barks of her wolf companions, which acted as watchdogs.

Hekate is the guardian not just of roads seen but of all journeys, including the journey to the afterlife. Her association with the Underworld and all its mystery led to her becoming the prominent goddess of witchcraft, magic, and sorcery, or so the contemporary tales tell it. However, for you here, in this moment, Hekate, like her early incantation "Bendis" the mother goddess, expresses her energy in its most authentic form as the custodian, cultivator, and protector of your most authentic self. Her energy, when called upon, adds a key ingredient to five particular parts of our life experience: our divine self, our needs as individuals, our intimate relationships, our role in the community, and our call to service.

The Five Pillars of Hekate

The "divine self" is you in purest energetic form; at your most innocent, your most neutral, your most unsullied, so to speak. It is the essence of you that comes from and remains connected to the creative force that pervades everything on this planet and beyond. Your only purpose is to radiate your energy, just like every star in our cosmos. Your divine self cannot exist on earth as you do, for it has no physical form, no plans, no mind of its own, and no emotional connections. Hekate's influence on our divine self helps us hold that energy within our bodies in physical form to protect it. It also allows us as emotional, physical beings to tap into the divine self's power as a reminder of our origin and our responsibility to use that energy as a force for creativity rather than destruction. Your own divinity can come under attack in this day and age from those who wish to control or have dominion over your life by seeking to pigeonhole you according to religion, or race, or gender.

The needs of the individual relate to your physical and emotional experience of this life. It relates to your basic needs like food, water, and shelter, and your need to explore your potential, talents, and desires in life. Hekate is a companion goddess for life if you need her to be, for the energy she can help you access directly or through your divine self is endless. Hekate's influence here extends to protecting your fundamental human rights, as well as your emotional and physical wellbeing. Also, you can call upon her energy to help guide you in times of doubt or dissolution, in times of seeking wisdom and counsel with regards to matters close to your heart and soul. The key to engaging Hekate for individual need is communication and honesty. When your intention is clear and for the purpose of betterment, many ways can be shown by Hekate, and many doors can be opened.

When it comes to your most intimate relationships, we look at immediate family and those we hold most dear. And as we have already discussed, these can be challenging and sometimes incredibly painful. They also present you with so many opportunities: to grow, to learn, to pass on your knowledge, to hold up a mirror to. These connections can even right wrongs of the past, clear karma, and heal ancestral lines. It sounds like a lot, but it needn't all be done at once or even in this lifetime. Consider the possibility that the people that play important parts in your life are not coincidentally there. Understanding what their role is in your life, what they have to offer or teach you, and what you are to them in return can make your journey multi-dimensional, one in which your emotions enhance your relationships rather than dictate them. Hekate's energy can protect you against difficulties by making you stronger, even enabling you to take a step back. Her keys can help unlock the mysteries of others' thoughts and intentions; her torches shine a light on things kept in the dark when you are ready to look. Her familiars, the wolves, can sense danger and warn you, in the same way as the story of her intervention in Byzantium.

The wider community within which you have influence is made up of all those people whom you "touch" with your presence, your energy: neighbours, work colleagues, school parents, teachers, coaches, shop assistants, your boss, employees, people you see through hobbies, or a sport. You make a connection with these people every time you come into contact in person, on the phone, even when emailing or texting. And they will connect with you. Most of the time, it will be fleeting, civil, even friendly, but sometimes it may not be. It is in these moments that you can call upon Hekate's energy to either give you the strength to speak out or to shield you.

Being shielded doesn't mean you are oblivious to what is being said or what is taking place; rather, its effect on you and the emotions it triggers in you are not detrimental to you—even if it means you are just able to hold it together long enough to get yourself to a more appropriate place to let rip if you need to. In my twenties, I often took myself off to the beach, a ten-minute drive from where I live, to walk along the shoreline and let my emotions out where they could do no harm; in fact, nine times out of ten, just being near the sea was enough for me to calm down or cheer up, whatever I needed. Though I didn't see it as Hekate's influence at the time, I knew and felt empowered that I had a safe way of dealing with confrontation and upset; the shoreline, the sea, and the sand were all part of my fortress.

Your call to service or a higher purpose can sound rather grandiose, but it is ultimately what every person is listening out for. This level of contentment may include understanding or even achieving "enlightenment"; for some, it may be related to financial security or emotional attachments. Perhaps it is about doing something "worthwhile" that impacts many people, even the world. And there is no shame in striving for them. So long as the ultimate feeling you experience along the way is a sense of being on the right track, then you are responding to your calling, whether you achieve the end result or not. Hekate will not give you all the answers, but she can help you prepare. It is her role as a holder of keys that comes to the fore. The keys (notice more than one) represent the various options before you and the many ways in which you can go about responding to your calling. You may even have more than one in a lifetime, especially if you have children or you are a primary carer.

◎ HAILING HEKATE INVOCATION

As you may now sense, there are many ways in which Hekate's energy can support and influence us: as a guardian, as a way-shower, and as one who can impart great wisdom and unlock the knowledge we have within. So now would be an excellent time to feel that energy for yourself and invite this wonderful goddess consciously into your presence through a simple but effective invocation.

YOU WILL NEED:

* A quiet space, where you can be seated at a table undisturbed for ten to fifteen minutes

* A small handheld bell for clearing

* Three candles: yellow (or gold) for direction, black for protection, and white for clarity of mind

* An object of power or significant meaning to you that you can hold in one hand or carry in a pocket; this could be a photo or picture, or something from your focal point

Begin by preparing the space; do this by clearing the area over the table and where you will be seated. Take your bell and ring it in the form of a cross over the table and around your chair. Place it down on the floor out of harm's way. Create a triangular space using the candles on the table with the gold candle at the top, the black candle to the left, and the white candle to the right. Finally, place your chosen object in the middle of the triangle. Now light all three candles starting with the black one, then yellow, and then white and set your intention; you can do this aloud or in your head, but simply say, *I call upon Hekate to share her energy with me today, for the greater good. Blessed be.*

So now we go about invoking her power in its three primary forms. Begin by focusing on the black candle and say, *Hail Hekate, Hail Hekate, Hail Hekate Empylios (Em-pee-lee-os), Guardian of Gates, share with me your energy that I may protect and preserve all that must be kept safe and secure, be it of thought, deed, or physical form.* Turn your attention now to the yellow candle and say, *Hail Hekate, Hail Hekate, Hail Hekate Lampidios (Lamp-a-dee-os), Bearer of Torches, share with me your energy that I may recognise and comprehend all the lessons and merits of each path before me, be it of thought, deed, or physical form.* Turn your attention now to the white candle and say, *Hail Hekate, Hail Hekate, Hail Hekate Kleidoukhos (Kl-eye-doe-kos), Keeper of Keys, share with me your energy that I may engage all my senses to act with clarity of vision and intention for the greater good.* Then finally focus on the object in the middle and say, *Hail Hekate Soteira (So-tee-era), Savior of Souls, with this object I call upon you for protection, guidance, and clarity, blessed be.*

Allow a minute or two for quiet contemplation, then blow out the candles. Your special object can either be carried on you as a talisman, should you require it, or you can place it back on your focal point or in a place of meaning to you in the knowledge that through it, you can call on Hekate's energy whenever you feel the need or just wish to be in that energetic presence. Put the candles and smudging tools away and go about your day.

This invocation is about a transfer of the goddess energy, in this case harnessing it in your power object or by transforming that object into a conduit for accessing Hekate's energy and gifts. However, some people may actually "see" Hekate manifest before them, which is nothing to be afraid of or feel confused about. Her appearance may be daunting, especially if you have been exposed to depictions of her looking "dark" and intimidating, with large wolves or black dogs flanking her. No goddess appears to cause harm; this creative power from the source of all life is neutral. You can influence it negatively or positively. Just as it is in life, what you put into this energy is what you will get out of it. The clearer your intentions, the more effective the energy will be. Keeping "good intentions"—that is to say, calling upon energy to work for the greater good, for a constructive outcome—is the most effective method we all possess in working to resolve issues with the assistance of the incredible goddesses within our reach. And Hekate, embodying the "triple goddess" within us all, adds a touch of magic.

Three Is a Magic Number

So much in life is looked at as two opposing sides: things being "black or white," "up or down," "right or wrong." It is considered a way to keep things simple or straightforward, but there is a whole other way in reality, the third option. Just think about a coin; when it is tossed, only "heads or tails" are the considered options, but every coin has a third side … the edge. "But it never lands on the edge," I hear you cry. But I would argue that doesn't mean the edge does not exist and cannot be explored; there is always a way forward or through. This triple aspect can be seen throughout all aspects of our existence: in religion as Father, Son, and Holy Ghost; in our experiences as past, present, and future; in our mortal phases of childhood, adulthood, and elderhood. And in our story telling of three little pigs or three bears, so it is no surprise that the goddess Hekate embraces the triple aspect of goddesshood: maiden, mother, and crone. The importance of three is at the core of our physical survival, too; it is dangerous to exceed three minutes without air, three days without water, or three weeks without food.

In building your own fortress, your resilient self, the power or rule of three can also be a great aid to restore order, set foundations, and give your purpose. Every day you can give yourself three things to accomplish. Naturally, you will do far more than that in a day, but you have a clear focus this way. For some, it may be to start a project that you have been putting off; it might be to compliment a stranger; it might be ensuring you get in touch with an old friend;

or something as simple as making the bed before you head out, or saying something positive to yourself in the mirror. At the end of the day, feel good about what you have accomplished. Even if you didn't get your things done, you will have learned something; maybe you need to give yourself more time, or undertake smaller tasks, or try a different approach to the task. But you will have focused attention on what you are doing, and with practice, you will get better at this and feel good about so many aspects of your day. Bit by bit, you will be building a stable, safe, and secure base from which you can tackle the world.

"Numerology" is the common term that encapsulates the belief in a mystical relationship between numbers and coinciding events, as well as the study of the numerical value of the letters, often associated with divinatory arts. The number 3 tarot card, for example, is the Empress, a card of creativity, a source of life that encourages an appreciation of natural beauty and artistry. In astrology, number 3 is linked to Gemini and Sagittarius's zodiac signs, both signs that embrace life to the full and thrive on shared ideas and positive experiences.

This belief in numbers has been traced back to the ancient civilisations of China, Greece, and the Middle East. The single digits, 1-9, are considered to have personality traits that set them apart from each other. By understanding what these traits are, it is believed we can unlock their messages. Often people can relate to seeing specific numbers over and over again, like 11:11, when looking at a clock randomly or waking up at a particular time, night after night. This is often taken as an opportune sign. In this context, the number 3, associated with all triple goddesses, speaks of communication, connection, and creativity.

This creative aspect is most linked with the youthful "maiden" aspect of Hekate. Calling on the maiden energy of Hekate is all about embracing life to the full, seeing it through rose-tinted glasses, and seeking out enjoyment wherever possible. This energy is of particular use if you feel down in the dumps, or lack joy or inspiration in your life, or if the modernity of your life has fenced you in. The Greeks associated this aspect of Hekate with Persephone, and so to tap into that youthful energy, you can say, *Hail Hekate, Hail Hekate, Hail Hekate Persephone, lift my head and straighten my back, fill me with the lust for life I lack. Let me be inspired by all the gifts you employ when you are residing in summer's joy.* However, it is worth noting that while it brings joy and excitement, the view of the world through rose-tinted glasses can also mask essential truths or harsher realities, so be sure not to get too caught up in frivolities or excesses without considering "the morning after" or longer-term consequences and being prepared.

If you are looking for a deeper connection with yourself, your higher self, or others, then it is to the "mother" aspect of Hekate that you can turn. Again keeping to the ancient Greeks' interpretation, the goddess Demeter, Persephone's mother, is associated with this part of Hekate's triple aspects. As you have already read, Demeter is one determined, driven, and potentially dangerous matriarchal figure. This energy fuels the drive to get to the root of all things, making her an excellent source to draw from when seeking to form or maintain strong bonds and relationships in life.

To energetically access that deep well of energy, you can say, *Hail Hekate, Hail Hekate, Hail Hekate Demeter, show me and the ones I love our common ground, and help to secure the connections we have found. Let our hearts entwine and our spirits soar, and may we remain in each other's thoughts evermore.* Being a magnet for others to be drawn to might at first make you feel incredible. Still, in life, it is about the quality of a relationship that really stands the test of time, rather than how many connections you have. So be a little selective and understand the investment it takes to form real, lasting bonds. Though the idea of committing to anything long-term can be daunting, it should not stop you from taking those initial steps. And this is particularly relevant to connecting more profoundly with yourself, getting to know all about who you are and what you really desire in life.

Then there is the culmination of all that the triple goddess Hekate is and understands in this life and beyond, which can be accessed through her wise woman or "crone" persona. With great age comes experience, knowledge, patience, empathy, and a desire to pass all this on. After all, what is the point of a wealth of knowledge if you cannot share it? This aspect of Hekate is most often misunderstood or much-maligned, just as most wise women—those with an understanding of plant medicine, the seasons, the animals, with honed intuitive skills, with a good appreciation and understanding of human nature too—have been throughout history. This is a well-crafted, well-preserved form of energy, and so it is both revered and feared: revered by those who appreciate its offerings and qualities, and feared by those who see it as a threat to their hold on power or control.

Again, your intention is what matters, and so with the right intention, you can access this tremendous energy by saying, *Hail Hekate, Hail Hekate, Hail Hekate, impart your wisdom and show me the way, that I might stand firm in my truth on this day. Let me see how far I have come and appreciate all I have thus far done.* Becoming wiser to the world around you and to the true intentions of the people around you, too, can be a bit of a double-edged sword. However, this is what the first steps to "enlightenment," to a greater sense of your spiritual self, uncover; it really isn't all about the acquisition of knowledge or power, but rather what you do with it and how you let it impact you. So be kind to yourself and others and use the wisdom of Hekate not just in the here and now but with a view of what is still to come.

You are not a two-dimensional being. Your life is not always as clear cut as you might like; along with the black and white, there is plenty of grey. You are required to make decisions all the time and have the conviction to stick by them. I am not just I. I am me, myself, and I. You are multi-dimensional, and as a creative being, you need to see life from many angles. Embracing the rule of three allows you to tap into an integral part of how you process, remember, and absorb information. We are geared to remember and connect with patterns, and three is the core of all patterns.

Through the triple goddess, her aspects, and talents, we can come to experience everything that life has to offer with greater courage and conviction. By embracing her energy, we discover what is important to us, our way forward through any situation, and we learn to protect and hold dear that which we believe. Three is a magic number, and as you come to understand that you are multi-dimensional, multi-faceted, you will see that you can make magic. Believe in yourself enough to stand your ground, and deliver to yourself what you believe in. This may put you at odds with other people, with society, but perhaps they are not living as they should.

Fortress of Your Creation

What would it feel like to be a fortress of your own creation? The process is about becoming closer to yourself, all parts of your life experience. You learn to face and embrace all aspects of yourself, which means extending that ethos to the areas you are not happy with. Love yourself enough to forgive, change, or reject those parts of your life. Your fortress will not be perfect, you may still avoid certain things initially about yourself or the things you have experienced, but over time, brick by brick, the opportunities will come to deal with that. If this is your first experience of "fortifying" your journey, you may have a few questions, like *Will I know how to be a strong person? How will I know who or what to let into my fortress? How can I deal with my past? Is happiness a real possibility for me? Does it even exist?*

There was a time when I questioned myself and the sense of trying to reconcile my past, manage my present, and create a better future. I had met plenty of "gurus," spiritual practitioners, and mortal people claiming to be "higher" beings, who all seemed to be somewhat unhappy behind closed doors or, worse, total hypocrites. But then I began to see that the idea of energy, of goddess resolutions, manifested itself in all sorts of people and all kinds of places. When I interviewed the actor, author, and seeker Shirley MacLaine years ago, I asked her if she actually liked people. She looked at me and smiled, much like my grandmother used to, and then leaned forward and told me what she really liked was the potential in people. And that is what building your fortress allows you to do: to access your potential by helping you manage and cope with your past and present.

So, how do you create your own fortress? Focus on approaching it with authenticity and honesty. Remember, once created, you will need to maintain it, stop it from crumbling to rubble. You do this by making a habit of visiting it, giving it a good spring clean, adding to it, or redecorating, so to speak. In your fortress, you come to better understand yourself by learning to accept the things you cannot change from the past but changing how they make you feel now. The new emphasis is on the present: how you can employ your emotions better, how you can unlock the opportunities and invite in the relationships that past experiences had made you avoid.

◎ Fortress Guided Visualisation

Your fortress offers a place where you can converse freely about your hopes and aspirations without the judgement or fears of others. Just as Rome wasn't built in a day, you will build your fortress in stages. I also know that we will have to stay diligent if we want our fortress to continue protecting us and offering sanctuary. From such a place, you stand strong in what you believe and ward off what you do not. It will be an ongoing effort, but one that is definitely worth the effort.

You will need:

* A quiet space, inside, at a table where you can sit comfortably undisturbed for fifteen to twenty minutes

* A single white candle in a holder and something to light it with

* Pen/pencil and paper

Begin by placing the candle on the table and sit down so you are comfortable and have a clear sight of the candle. Now light the candle and focus on the flame, breathing normally, just focus on the flame allowing all other images or thoughts to drift away. Notice how the flame appears, brighter on the outside and darker in its centre; just focus and breathe normally for a few moments and then, when you feel ready to, close your eyes. You will see the flame's image appear in your mind's eye; it may be a different colour but that is fine. Just hold that image and relax into your seated position. Take three deep breaths, in through the nose and out through the mouth, and gently allow the image of the flame to transform into an image of your fortress. This is your place of resilience, security, authenticity, and power. See it rise from the ground, rock by rock. Continue to breathe slowly but gently; with each breath, your fortress is becoming taller and more defined. It may have a deep moat around it, full of glistening water, with a massive drawbridge or a large pair of solid wooden doors. Your fortress is not impenetrable, but you get to decide who and what may come in.

Your fortress may have just one single tower or several; it may have one or two windows or even many; it is up to you how you wish to construct the image. But as you do, remember, this is not a place of imprisonment, but a place that represents the core of you, your beliefs, your ideas, your values. Allow this fortress to reflect that through colour or shape; perhaps you now see magnificent vines or climbing flowers encase the outer walls. Hints of old wild roses or exotic jasmine briefly fill the air. You may notice great woodlands appear around the fortress, or if you prefer, you may have your fortress perched high on a mountain or cliff edge with incredible far-reaching views. Allow this magnificent place to flourish before you. Continuing to breathe, you notice a path extend out from your fortress and see yourself now walking to the entrance along this path.

You enter with ease, and a sense of coming home flows through you as you stand in the entrance hall. This is a vast magnificent space, decorated with all the imagery that you delight in. You are safe and welcome here at any time. You look around you again and notice three passageways: one to your right, another to your left, and the third in front of you. These passageways are open to you at any time and serve an important purpose. Turn to face the left and head along that passageway; it feels familiar, and your nose is filled with scents from your childhood, the food you liked, the smell of a favourite place, and you can hear voices too, from your past. There is no need to fear; even though you may encounter things from your past that hurt or upset you, they can do you no harm now.

As you enter the chamber, you will see elements from your past that are both positive and negative. The negative experiences and people are but small stone statues in this room on a shelf. Their sole purpose now is a reminder of what you don't need, of behaviours that no longer serve you. All the good things from your past dance and delight before your eyes, taking the form of a glorious bed upon which you can rest, beautiful lights, beautiful books filled with the moments of your past that make you smile. This is your heart space. Turn now and step out of this chamber to you find yourself back in the entrance hall, standing as you were when you came in. Now turn to your right and follow that passage.

Walking along this passage, you have a strong sense of being very much in the here and now. The voices you can hear and what you can smell remind you of your life right now, and as you come to the chamber, you realise it a representation of your life as it is now. There are photos of the people in your life at this moment. The table and chairs before you look like those from your kitchen or dining room, the sofa is your sofa, and there is music playing that is the music you are enjoying at this moment in your life. There is a large window, and as you look out, you have the same view that you do from your current living room.

This is your present. And as you look around you more carefully again, you notice photos of people who make you feel a little uncomfortable; you see some of the furniture is looking a little worn. These are the indicators of what needs to be worked on at this time in your life: relationships that need to change or end, things you need to let go of; they may relate to work, to friends, to yourself even. But in this chamber, you have the time and space to explore these options and make plans. This is your headspace. Turn now and step out of this chamber, and you find yourself back in the entrance hall, standing just as you were when you came in. Now walk straight ahead along the third passage.

This passage is lighter and feels colder than the other two, it is quiet in comparison, but you feel exhilarated. As you enter the chamber, it is as if your thoughts and desire and best outcomes for your future hopes and dreams are projected onto the blank wall around you. They are slightly faded and almost shimmering. You focus on one image; it is like a short film of your best dream about your future is being premiered before you, and it showcases all the possible outcomes. You are almost taken aback by the detail and what can be achieved in your life. You look now at the large table in the room, and on it are blank sheets of paper and a selection of pens and pencils. You feel the desire to just take a seat and create; it may be in poetry or drawings or a simple written account of your dreams for tomorrow or next week, next year. Here you are free to create, to manifest, and to experiment with your potential. This is your soul space.

When you are ready to leave this chamber, follow the passage back to the hall. When you reach the hall, take three deliberate breaths in through the nose, out through the mouth, and gradually come back to your authentic self. Let any visions of the chambers and the fortress fade. Allow your breathing to return to normal and open your eyes. Blow out the candle on the table and, taking the pen and paper you have at hand, make a note of the outstanding visions and moments from visiting each of the chambers in your fortress. This will be a way of ordering where you need to focus your day-to-day energy. This is how Hekate's power can work with you to effect real change and grow in your life. Perhaps it's something unresolved from the past or something you want to explore more of in the future... Then, ensure that you address those things over the next few days or weeks.

Becoming the Fortress, Resolution Tips

The older we get, the more we put ourselves "out there," the more we interact with others, the more situations present themselves for us to demonstrate conviction of thought and words. And it can be hard to find that backbone, plant our feet, and stand our ground. How often do you stand up for yourself or what you know to be true, especially in the face of ardent opposition? Probably not as often as you should. Most people try to get through each day, avoiding conflict as much as possible, which is an admirable thing to do. Still, it can also result in a person giving their power away; they are not standing their ground but allowing other people to bulldoze it all up. It can feel really uncomfortable to be assertive sometimes, and these tense situations can bring to light painful memories and deep-seated feelings of insecurity or inadequacy. And the more trauma a person has suffered in their past, the more likely they will give way to others' needs and wants to avoid it. Sadly, this just creates more trauma because they are not being true to themselves and eventually will become victims all over again. Being assertive doesn't mean being a tyrant or being aggressive; it means having confidence in your feelings' authenticity and the validity of your worth. So take stock and remember...

Understanding how we create a circle of protection and why we do it connects us again to the purest energies that we can then use when working with the energies of other people, places, and situations.

The core principles of stoic practice—including preparation, self-control, and self-care—keep us on the path to wellbeing without being distracted too easily or too often by instant gratification or the fear of being hurt. Practice the Pillar of Discernment Ritual as often as you need to, to help you regulate your principles, connecting with various elements' energies.

The goddess Hekate is the multi-dimensional embodiment of womanhood, from innocent to protector to wisdom-keeper. But it is in her original role as "mother" that she comes to you in this chapter to help you make sense of your life so far, restore some order and a sense of purpose, and give you the determination to stand by all of it.

The act of calling upon a deity for aid, protection, or inspiration is also a form of prayer invoking the presence of creative energy, so calling upon the powers associated with Hekate not only channels all she has to offer but awakens those aspects within ourselves. We call for help, but at the same time must be willing to help ourselves too.

It is often said that "all good things come in threes," an expression that transcends both pagan and monastic beliefs. The practice of looking at life from three perspectives rather than just one or two that are often in opposition grants more insight and time to consider our options, and therein lies the magic of this number.

Guided visualisations help open up the possibilities of your creative power. They can offer you the time and space to gently and safely organise and make sense of complicated issues, overwhelming tasks, or grand undertakings.

CHAPTER 8
Picking Your Battles

J ust as there are times to stand in your power and in your truth, there will also be times to "right wrongs." Despite our best efforts to do otherwise, a need for redemption or atonement must be fulfilled. This is a need driven by all manner of injustices. It is time to look at this need and how it can best be managed, even how and when to execute these actions. Being selective about the arguments or confrontations that you involve yourself with in the first place means you can save time and energy for those things that really matter, because not everything warrants a fight. Looking into the future, say in a few years from now, it is clear that a lot of your current concerns and worries will fade. And every battle you look to fight, every problem you immerse yourself in, every crisis that keeps you awake at night, saps you of energy. Once you have won, you might also wonder whether your time could have been better spent on something else.

Warrior Goddesses of the Hemispheres

The lessons we can learn from the myths surrounding the Haitian goddess Maman Brigitte and the jotunn hunter goddess Skadi from Norse mythology are compelling. The lessons within these myths add to our emotional armoury. Like any martial art teaches, the more you learn about and how to use your "weapons" correctly, the less likely you will feel a need to. These two goddesses come from two directions of great strength and power. Maman Brigitte is supported by the south and Skadi by the north. These directions function best when both are present in equal measure. As with so much that involves energy and wellbeing, balance is what we strive for. And so resolving conflict should be about retaining the balance, whether that be through the transfer of power, righting a wrong, taking responsibility, accepting failure, or seeing justice done. The north and the south's energies are often the most predominant or influential when people clash, so understanding them can provide great insight and relief when tensions run high.

Remember, your life isn't about "winning," it's about making the best use of your time. Do you want to spend your life pondering over every argument, worrying about every foe you might encounter? Your journey should be about how well your life is created and lived, about the people you love, and about your impact on the world around you. So, when it comes to picking your battles, be strategic; taking on every cause in life means you will have little time or energy for anything else. There is a fine line between knowing when to take something further and when to turn away, especially when our emotions are running riot and the urge to act becomes almost overwhelming. This is particularly true when tempers are heated, and so we look to the lessons of our first goddess, Maman Brigitte.

Southern Heat with Maman Brigitte

When we say that "hell hath no fury like a woman scorned," it usually means that there is no anger greater than a woman who has been rejected in love. The proverb is adapted from *The Mourning Bride*, a play by William Congreve, but it could also be a calling card for one of the most down-to-earth goddesses you will learn about. Maman Brigitte, like some of her global counterparts Brigid (Celtic), Pele (Pacific), and Oya (African), is a fire goddess. These goddesses of strength, passion, and courage are fearless warrior deities who do not tolerate the whimsical, the self-absorbed, or those who seek to inflict harm. They help to move us forward physically and emotionally, teaching us about strength and courage and giving us a voice to speak our truth and be reckoned with.

Legend has it that Maman Brigitte is Baron Samedi's partner and a highly respected intermediary between mortals and the divine. She is most often associated with death, the Underworld, and the protection of women, particularly when it comes to domestic violence, infidelity, sexually transmitted diseases, fertility issues, and childbirth. If called upon to assist, nothing can escape her cleansing flames. She actively and with force deals out punishment.

This force in her is only matched by her abilities to heal, which includes midwifery of the soul, i.e., if someone suffers from long-term illness, Maman Brigitte can step in and heal or ease their suffering by ending their mortal existence and ensuring the safe transition of the soul. As guardian of the dead, she is said to appear in cemeteries to bless the graves, and deals harshly with those who fail to respect the dead, hence the reason it is a Haitian custom to dedicate the first woman to be buried in a new cemetery to Maman Brigitte.

Those who claim to have seen her describe her as of seductive flesh and bone, oozing sex appeal and dressed in layers of purple and black or purple and green, sometimes laced in white trim. The garments are pinched in at the waist and low cut off with her midriff exposed, accentuating her womanly curves, and often she wears a striking black top hat adorned with feathers. Her colourful garments are matched by her equally colourful language. Partial to offerings of rum and hot peppers, she can swear and cuss with the best of them to make her point, show her displeasure, or ward off unwanted energy. She demands that women be treated with respect by their partners, and women often call on her to seek redemption when they are wronged. In essence, this deity represents the inherent need for loyalty to preserve mind, body, and soul as a sacred right, and a fundamental desire to be treated as the divine beings we all are.

Lessons of Maman Brigitte

In picking our battles, the lessons of Maman Brigitte take on two roles. The first is about the fighting spirit that helps us speak up and see the confrontation through, especially if we are naturally drawn to relinquish our position, or are seen as easy targets. And secondly, she takes on the role of the redeeming healer, which may take several different forms. We will now explore both of these roles and their value to us when we face conflict. As a fire goddess, Maman Brigitte's energy can help us vocalise what we feel, need, and want. So, I ask you now if you have ever felt utterly incapable of speaking your truth? Perhaps this manifested itself like a physical barrier stopping the words being spoken from the heart ever reaching your mouth?

I remember vividly, as a child of three or four years of age, sitting outside my parents' bedroom for what seemed like half the night, too afraid to go in and tell them I was having terrible nightmares and hearing things. I didn't want to frighten my mother, and I was in fear of disappointing my father. And on the odd occasion, I did disturb them. I couldn't bring myself to say why and would just put it down to not being able to settle. But I was fortunate; I had supportive parents, and even though they were busy with work and looking out for my baby brother, I had grandparents that doted on me and encouraged me to express myself. They were great storytellers, happy to share their memories, views, and feelings and, best of all, they had time to listen to me, so I grew older with a passion for communication. There is definitely a bit of Maman Brigitte's fire in my belly when I need to have my say.

Speaking your truth with grace is one way of navigating your way through an ever-changing world filled with complicated people and the battles that ensue. It is worth considering that deceit, lies, and half-truths require a lot of energy to exist and maintain, whereas the truth requires no more effort once it is expressed. With her sharp mind and quick tongue, Maman Brigitte just says it exactly as it is, and taking on some of her energy can help you do the same. As she is associated with the element of fire, one of her talents is to incinerate what is not right and leave only that which is.

By practising to speak your truth and the more difficult truths in life (for, as the saying goes, "truth hurts"), you can learn to do it with compassion. By that, I mean you can do it from a place of wanting to ease a situation rather than prolong something based on fabrication, which can be far more painful in the long run. Honesty is the best policy, if not always the most well-received. You may be afraid to speak up or take action to reveal the truth because it goes against our natural, tribal instincts to not alienate ourselves from others. But in not speaking up or taking action, we create division within and alienate ourselves.

In contrast, when sharing a brutal truth, we regain alignment with our true selves and the cosmos's creative forces. We feel better for it, and going back to our old ways is not an appealing option. We take a good look at all aspects of our lives and relationships and have a good clear-out, embracing the opportunity to be honest with others and true to ourselves. This may see the end of relationships, a career change, or what you are prepared to do for others, setting boundaries. It may also mean expressing your true feelings, telling people you love them, for example, letting your guard down. The more you do this, the more you restore harmony within and attain emotional equilibrium.

The theological notion of redemption weighs heavily on most people because it stems from being used chiefly when apportioning fault or blame in others. A radical, more holistic approach calls for a deeper understanding. The main focus is not merely about apportioning blame but remembering that redemption, bringing things back into alignment, should be made possible, even when we feel incapable of addressing the pain or suffering caused by the conflict. In this way, redemption becomes a tool for greater healing that enables us to free ourselves, not condemn others. You may wonder why some negative or destructive patterns in your life keep repeating, like continually choosing the wrong partner, having reoccurring money issues, losing one job after another, or having the same arguments with members of your family.

Maman Brigitte exerts her healing powers through her actions of redemption on an emotional and energetic level by forcing people to bear witness to the suffering and conflict they have caused or been a part of and then, more importantly, giving them the opportunity to make amends. She may employ rather direct tactics, bordering on violence, or some that are very cunning. But at the heart of all of this is a need to get to the truth, the root cause, heal it, learn from it, and prevent the whole thing from occurring time and time again.

And sometimes, to uncover experiences and events that have been buried for years, Maman Brigitte will unleash the cleansing power of fire. This might manifest itself in all your emotions coming to the fore, and you verbally release the frustration, anger, pain, or confusion you have been holding within. It may result in material damage, and in self-defence, you could get physical. We want to pre-pare against the latter unless you are fighting for your life or against sexual aggression. The thing to remember is that whatever you do, however you engage Maman Brigitte's energy in your life, she will be looking back at you also. Again, as with all goddess work, the intention is fundamental. Set your intention always for the greater good and act with integrity and honesty when you seek the help of Maman Brigitte or tap into her energy. Because if you don't follow the rules of engagement with such a powerful and emotional fire goddess, you will get your fingers burnt and possibly worse.

Exploring the South with Maman Brigitte

The direction of the south is the gateway to the physical realm; it teaches us what it really means to be a creative force inside a phys-ical body. Being associated with the summertime of the year, this direction helps us to be emotionally grounded and accepting of the physical limitations that being in your own skin represents. This is about integrating what we learn and manifest in our thoughts and expressing it through our actions and outer appearance. Just as summer is characterised by change and rapid growth, you also experience growth when engaged with the south.

On our journey as adolescents, that type of rapid growth is experienced in the body and mind. We begin to learn to judge and value, taking our first steps along the path of discernment but still relying on dualistic "black and white" thinking when it comes to judgement. The south is still governed by passion, innocence, and a certain level of ignorance in which the multi-faceted complexities of adulthood and multiple truths of reality are not yet integrated. We experience things more one-dimensionally, and the kinds of relationships explored will be about love and romance. There is also the struggle with rebellion that conformity brings, and all of these challenges of human life continue into adulthood.

When we are around forty or fifty years old, the "midlife crisis" is simply a returning to the youthful energies of the south as our inner life and development continue in the cycle whether we are conscious of it or not. Rather than trying to fight, look to cooperate with natural processes consciously. By understanding lessons of the south energies, we can choose our response to this natural part of human life more effectively. The south is also the place of healing, for ourselves and for the dense materiality of the Earth plane. Being matter, both are susceptible to damage or destruction. We are tasked with keeping our physical body whole and healthy so it can be a stable vehicle for the soul.

◎ Guided Journey to the South

This visualisation is an appropriate preparation in times of confrontation that requires action. The fire in your belly needs to be stoked to burn through the walls of resistance that you will meet in the battle ahead. Fighting fire with fire can get everyone burnt, so consider using this energy carefully; it must be something really worth fighting for. And then we need to be equally ready to heal and repair. Both are attributes found when working with the energy and goddesses of the south.

You will need:

* A quiet space inside where you can lie down undisturbed for fifteen to twenty minutes

* A red candle and something to light it with

Having selected your quiet space, face south. Now call to the direction by saying, "*Hail and welcome the energy of the south, give me the courage and allow me to see, the healing that must be done to strengthen me.*" Now light your candle, focus briefly on the flame, and place it safely in the most southerly part of your space, then return to the middle of your space and lie down in a position that is most comfortable to you. Close your eyes and take three deep breaths in through the nose and out through the mouth, and relax further, allowing yourself to gently drift, focusing your mind's eye on the red flame flickering in the distance. Continue to take deliberate, steady breaths; if it feels more relaxing, you can breathe in and out through mouth or nose or a combination; just be sure to breathe deeply and relax.

Using your mind's eye, allow the red flame to gradually expand and fill your vision, so you are surrounded by a warm, soft red light. And as you take in this light, notice it gradually fading to reveal a dense area of tropical forest, through which strands of light penetrate the rich green leaves and twisted vines all around you. You hear exotic bird calls, and in the background, you can hear what sounds like the ocean. You notice there is a well-worn path ahead of you, and so you now follow it, towards the sound of the waves. As you walk along, feeling warm and almost overwhelmed by the rich diversity of plant life and colour, you can see ahead a break in the vegetation and the sight of a white sandy beach and blue water come into view.

As you emerge onto the beach, you are struck by the healing sea breeze and, turning to your left, you see a wooden beach hut; smoke is coming from a vent in the roof and all around it is a large verandah and what looks like an occupied hammock, swinging in the breeze. There are wooden barrel planters of various sizes everywhere, some filled with lavender, some with ferns, some fruit trees, and some with a mix of flowers and vegetables. Your eyes are drawn to the front door, which appears to be open, enticing you in. And within the blink of an eye, you find yourself standing on the bottom step of the verandah of this curious dwelling. As you step up, the wood creaks slightly, almost as if it were saying "hello."

You turn to your right and notice the figure in the hammock looks very familiar even under the large sun hat. It's you. And with this realisation, the reclining you turns their head up to you and smiles while gesturing with an outstretched hand for you to look back out over your shoulder at the view of the sea. As you turn around, you notice that the palm trees, the large planters, and the beach are teeming with life. Bees take turns dipping in the lavender, all manner of colourful birds rest in the trees or dance in the breeze, the ocean waves glisten as they come to the shore and then retreat again as if the whole vast body of water is breathing right before your very eyes. All this expression of life is soul-soothing.

You turn back to the door now and choose to step inside. You are in the space of genuine wonder. To your right is a large hearth, with an old black pot hanging over an open fire, tended to by a shapely woman, dressed in layers of black and purple; she beckons you to look around. To your left is what looks like a beautifully hand-crafted kitchen, with a large window above the white marble sink. Beyond a large round table is a massive dresser filled with all manner of jars and bottles, almost all of which are full of lotions or liquids of various colours, or dried leaves and herbs. You now take a few more

steps in so you can look in more detail at the table. It has
books and pieces of old papers piled high on one side. There
are recipes, manuals, diaries, books on plants and animals,
books about healing, and even a few cookbooks. You can see
they are well-used and well-loved. It now hits you: the smells
of essential oils, natural soaps, and drying herbs suspended
from the beams above. Breathe these in and out slowly and
let their healing properties seep into you. Now, as you walk
around the table towards the dresser, you notice little wooden
doors on either side. Both are ajar.

You go through the door to the left of the dresser to find
yourself in a square room with workbenches on three sides.
And on these workbenches are all the ingredients, tools, and
containers you could ever need to prepare tinctures, salves,
oils, lotions, and potions for looking after the body, mind,
and spirit. There is a large window that runs along the bench
to your left, and it is open to allow the summer breeze in. As
you look out of this window, you see what looks like children
at play on the beach; they chase each other, collecting driftwood and shells and laughing. And you recall all your happy
times as a child. You turn your attention back to the room
and now look out of the window that runs the bench's length
on the back wall. And there, a little farther away, you can see
out onto a lagoon, and on the jetty and in the water, you see
young adults enjoying themselves; swimming, bathing in the

warm sun, embracing each other. And you recall what young love and youthful exuberance felt like.

You now turn back around and leave this room, step back into the main room, and walk into the room on the other side of the dresser. Immediately you take a deep breath of lavender air in and feel yourself relaxing further. You are in a most beautiful room with light coming in from the window at the back, and to your right is a glorious four-poster bed made of driftwood, decorated with seashells and fine white netting gathered at the corners. This bed invites you to lie down, and you do. The bedding is crisp and sweet-smelling, large plump pillows cushion your head, and the mattress is just to your liking. As you lie there taking in the room, you notice in one corner what looks like a staff, adorned with shells and what could either be coloured glass or crystals; next to it is an impressive broom, and on the shelves to the side, there are neatly arranged feather fans, sage bundles, and a stack of abalone shell halves. You realise that this place of healing and repair is also a place of summoning power and energy. Here you are with all the tools and energy you could ever need to create, defend, and recover.

You can engage with whomever you choose, learn about healing, or just play in the sea under the sun or rest in the hammock in the breeze; it is all here for you. With all this access to a place of joy and healing, of freedom and play, to fill you with positivity and desire, you can spend as much time as you like now in this direction of the south. When you are ready, see yourself getting up from the bed and walking through the cottage to the entrance doors, and step out into the summer sun with the sea breeze on your face and, looking ahead, notice a small red flame flickering. Watch it as it expands to fill your vision and then gently fades as you slowly open your eyes. Allow yourself a little time to come into the present moment, gently rise, and go and blow out the candle.

If you already have a hot temper, or you are quick to rise to a challenge, or you are too often led by your emotions rather than you managing them, then perhaps you are already dancing a little close to the fire. Maybe you have become too reliant or too well-acquainted with Maman Brigitte, and you would be better to seek the more calculating composure of a goddess of winter instead. Holding fire in check, on the other side of the compass is a deity less of mortal realms; she is a giant among giants, and I suggest now would be a good time to step out of the fire and see the view from a very different perspective.

On the Shoulder of a Giant

If ever there was a goddess whose might you would want on your side in an altercation, one who is skilled in hunting, has incredible stamina, understands the lay of the land, and also understands the natural world and its powers, then that is the goddess who awaits you now. Skadi (Skah-dee) is the Norse jotunn (giant) goddess of winter, hunting, and skiing, who rules over the mountains and wilderness. The almighty Asgard god Odin described her home, the grand hall Thrymheim, as the "ancient court," a place high in the mountains where she presides as judge, jury, and executioner settling any type of confrontation, injustice, or imbalance of power. Although Skadi is a giant and associated with the many facets of winter like long dark nights, the cold, and even death, there is a benevolence about her that makes her stand out from her race and undeniably approachable.

There are many stories about Skadi, but the following best exemplify the qualities we seek in her. The first shows her determination and self-worth, triggered by her father's death at the hands of Odin. Skadi's father, the giant Thiazi, dares to kidnap the beautiful goddess of youth, Idun. And in doing so, he takes the gods' apples of immortality. Odin kills Thiazi and rescues Idun. Skadi is enraged at Odin's drastic action and seeks to avenge her father. She takes her weapons, including her notorious hunting bow, and singlehandedly storms the citadel of Asgard and demands compensation for her father's loss, or she will inflict her vengeance on all the gods. She gives the gods a choice of either a benign or harmful consequence. In fear of the mighty Skadi, the gods offer her gold, but gold means little to Skadi, who has plenty of riches already from her ancestors' pillaging over the years.

So Odin offered her goddess status among the Asgardians by letting her pick a husband from among the gods. She agrees, hoping to bag herself the handsome Baldur, whom she had taken a shine to, but there was one condition. Odin would only let her pick a god by the look of his shoes, and Skadi ended up with Njord, the god of the sea, because his shoes were best. Unsurprisingly, the marriage didn't last more than a couple of weeks; Njord couldn't tolerate the mountains' bitter cold, and Skadi couldn't bear the bright sunshine and warmth of the coast. So, they parted ways, and Skadi returned to Asgard demanding a suitable husband, this time of her choosing. She marries none other than Odin himself, and they go on to have many children.

The second story relates to Skadi attending a great feast. She hears the two gods Loki and Heimdallr speaking, and interjects, warning Loki to hold his wayward tongue. She then leans in to tell him that his abusive and reckless behaviour towards the goddesses is about to end, for soon the gods will bind Loki to a sharp rock with the entrails of his own son. In true predatory form, Loki sneers and remarks that Skadi was far more friendly towards him when they were in bed together, something he says of all the goddesses. He has gone too far now, and it is not long before he is caught and bound with the innards of his murdered son. Skadi holds a venomous snake above Loki's face, its venom dripping into a bowl held by Loki's wife Sigyn. But when the basin is full and is removed to be emptied, the snake venom drips onto Loki's face and causes such excruciating pain that his violent writhing sends earthquakes through the land as he atones for his wrongdoings.

Our battles can be just as much about coping with the after-effects of "fighting the good fight." By that, I mean assuring that justice is done, that the balance of power is restored, and that some form of reconciliation is reached. This is what atonement from Skadi's energetic perspective is about.

Atonement in Action

People can act without thinking, give way to unhealthy emotions, and say things they really don't mean to say when under duress or threatened. Passions can run high at times, and balance or perspective is lost. Having strong feelings can be a positive driving force, like seeking out the truth, working hard, and getting things done. Still, strong feelings can also lead to conflict, and this can be significantly heightened when the people you have a connection with actually take a different view. Skadi's influence is about taking the heat out of the situation, remaining calm, even calculating, by clearly and pragmatically spelling out the consequences of either behaviour that causes harm or unresolved conflict.

Things can quickly escalate to argumentative behaviours, fights, and even the destruction of relationships for those who don't know how to resolve a dispute. Further hardships can arise when you are not prepared to cope with the consequences of these battles of body, mind, and soul. Atonement, in the form that we employ supported by Skadi's energy, is about making things right after the event and providing essential steps along the way to resolve a conflict. The measures may seem simple enough; however, they are not always easy to take. I ask you to bear in mind that the aim is for these coping strategies to lead to a more supportive and collaborative way of navigating these complex situations, one that may also mean we can avoid unpleasant consequences altogether.

When situations begin to come to a head, or you sense unease brewing, keep the lines of communication open. Things will be so much more difficult to resolve if you can't agree to talk in a civilised way, without interruptions, with respect, without shouting or swearing or insulting each other. Agreeing to talk, along with guidelines that are supportive and hold a safe space for all, is the start of finding a resolution to a conflict. And with that in mind, establishing some basic ground rules gives the conversation a better chance of being productive and making all parties involved feel comfortable to share their side of things. You can now begin to talk about what is going on, one side at a time. Everyone must continue to follow the guidelines because emotions can still be raw, and people will have a desire to express themselves and may want to interrupt. But by following the ground rules set out, it should be easier for each person to share their point of view without argument. If each person can explain their position while staying calm and respectful, it will greatly increase the chance of finding a resolution.

With communication lines open, clearly identifying the problem or conflict is a significant next step that can often be overlooked. It helps if each party can talk about what they see as the root cause of the problem. And being able to do this succinctly, with just a sentence or two, helps us avoid getting caught up in our emotions rather than looking at the facts. Many people can get swept up by their emotions, especially when feeling vulnerable, defensive, fearful, or not being heard, often elements that make up conflict. It is easy to lose sight of what the conflict is really about in this state of mind. Therefore, by identifying the issue in simple terms, it keeps everyone focused on the problem and looking forward to resolving it rather than going off on emotionally fueled tangents that run the risk of the whole process breaking down. Now we look to move forward by all parties taking it to offer up ways of resolving things. This is about exploring the options at this stage. The ideas and suggestions for resolving the conflict might require compromise, so just for now, consider all of it rather than seeing the concessions as a cause for further aggravation. Right now, you are only looking at what might happen, so remain open and respectful. From this perspective, it will be much easier to actually find an agreement.

Now comes the time to discuss which idea might make the most sense in the circumstances, or which has the best chance of resolving the matter, or the idea that everyone can agree upon. This is not the time for digging in your heels, breathing fire, or trying to exert your will. Put the emotions attached to the situation aside, don't dwell on the past, no matter how painful, and instead focus on what will resolve the conflict effectively for all. When you have a solution, say it aloud to ensure all parties clearly understand and agree. In time you may want to revisit this particular outcome; for example, the solution today might be to go separate ways, and you will have to decide then when who takes what and so on. So it is useful in those circumstances to arrange when you will next speak or meet up again.

As has been said, this is a process, and there may be a few steps of "atonement" to take even after the initial "battle" comes to an end. Keeping a cool, clear head in times like this can be the difference between actually moving things forward or making necessary changes and all-out war. This process can be incredibly useful, and once you learn when and how to implement it, you will feel much more confident about resolving a conflict when one arises. This process has the added benefit of improving communication skills, skills that, when applied in our day-to-day life, can often prevent misunderstandings, arguments, and more in the first place. These communication skills are essential in all our relationships, helping us communicate effectively and honestly, traits the goddess Skadi had in abundance.

Lessons of the North

The north is where we live and express ourselves out of our most authentic nature. We all know people who live transparent, honest lives, who are genuinely themselves even if others don't like them or approve of their ways. What is so attractive about these people is that they are real. They do not play social and political games to be liked or to stay safe. They address life on life's terms and don't spend their precious energy trying to manipulate or change their circumstances by blaming others or victimising themselves. We turn to people of the north in times of crises and emergencies because we can count on them to be fully present. They are available to those who genuinely need them, and they have clear boundaries for themselves and others. They are neither arrogant nor prideful but are assured and confident in their sense of their soul knowing. They are our teachers and leaders because we can trust them, their natures, and their behaviour.

The energy of the north encourages us to take full responsibility for all aspects of our life, including our words and deeds. As the dwelling place of teachers, ancestors, and wisdom-keepers, the north is no place for those playing the victim or for those who cannot or will not accept the reality of what their thoughts and emotions can create. Being a responsible person does not mean you have to take on all the world's dilemmas and make them your own. Instead, it means you should be aware of what you are doing, like what you post on social media, say to a family member, or how you behave in the wider world. Hold yourself to account for your actions; avoid apportioning blame for your actions on others. Working with energy, creating your life, and walking your path will mean you make mistakes, but the errors are opportunities to say or do something differently next time. Not learning from your mistakes, not taking responsibility, is the real waste of your time and energy.

The north is also the place of acceptance, where you can be who you are—the good, the bad, and the ugly—because the wisdom that resides here helps us know, understand, and accept who we are: our talents, our potential, and our individual limitations. It encourages us to peer beneath the surface and observe what is pure, authentic, and productive in others, in a situation and within our own being. The ability to respond to an "attack" or to a conflicting situation with a clearer head, and the vision to see beyond and all the possible outcomes, result from knowing that we can control how we deal with adversity and how it affects us.

◎ Guided Journey to the North

This visualisation is about engaging with the direction of the north, Skadi's territory, where wisdom is sought to get answers. It will help you identify the truth and the motivations so that you can either atone for your part or get the atonement you seek. It is also a way of preparing you to accept the truth and allow you to move forward without attaching any negative feelings to the outcome. It can be undertaken whenever you feel the need for wisdom, to find a place of sanctuary and peace, and to reside in the energy of those who have gone before or all of the knowledge you have gained from your experiences in this lifetime. It is a place of contemplation and consideration. When it comes to picking your battles, the north is the place of the wise counsel.

You will need:

* A quiet space inside where you can lie down undisturbed for fifteen to twenty minutes
* A white candle and something to light it with

Having selected your quiet space, face north. Now call to the direction by saying, *Hail and welcome the energy of the north, reveal the truth and allow me to see what the challenges ahead have to teach me.* Now light your candle, focus briefly on the flame, and place it safely in the most northern part of your space, then return to the middle of your space and lie down in a position that is most comfortable to you. Close your eyes and take three deep breaths in through the nose and out through the mouth, and relax further, allowing yourself to gently drift, focusing your mind's eye on the white flame flickering in the distance. Continue to take deliberate, steady breaths; if it feels more relaxing, you can breathe in and out through mouth or nose or a combination; just be sure to breathe deeply and relax. Using your mind's eye, allow the white flame to expand and fill your vision so you are surrounded by cool, soft white light.

As you take in this light, notice it gradually fading to reveal a large, impressive, pale grey stone building looming before you. Even though it is dark outside, you can make out that its turrets are covered in snow, and the arched windows are closed, but here and there, candlelight illuminates them from within. You notice it is snowing, but so gently that it barely makes a sound. Straight ahead is a large wooden door adorned with intricate metalwork. It is slightly ajar, drawing you in. You take a few steps forward and enter this incredible building...

Inside now, you are in a great hall; down either side are bookshelves, full of books, scrolls, and manuscripts of various sizes, colours, and ages. There is a large wooden table that runs almost the length of the room; at the far end, you can see an enormous stone hearth, with a fire burning and a large comfy chair to one side, in which a person is seated and reading. As you walk along the hall, past the shelves towards the hearth, you can see the person seated is actually you. You look at your seated self, they look at you and you both smile. To the left of the hearth, there is an archway. You now walk through, entering a smaller room, filled with golden three-dimensional geometric shapes, some hanging from the ceiling, some on plinths, and to your right there are a couple of wide, stone steps up to a sizeable golden telescope framed by a massive window with an uninterrupted view of the night sky.

Another, smaller archway is to your left and leads you to a third room; this is warm and inviting; tapestries and portraits hang from the walls, and large candle chandeliers hang from the ceiling and light the room. There are plush settees and comfortable armchairs arranged around a big stone fireplace with a fire crackling within. You can see the glow of the fire now on the faces of all the people seated in this room; some look familiar, some you have never seen before, but all of them are welcoming, and you enter this room feeling totally at ease. Surrounded by these people, in the welcoming, warm space, you can ask anything, for this is your place of sanctuary, of gaining awareness, of respite from your everyday busy life. Here you are with the ancestors, with the wisdom keepers, with your past journeys and all the knowledge and wisdom this direction holds.

You can engage with whomever you choose, or pore over the books and scripts in the library hall, or gaze upon the stars; you have access to it all. Encompassed by all this knowledge to fill you with confidence and assurance, you can spend as much time as you like now in this direction of the north. When you are ready, see yourself walking through the building to the entrance doors and stepping out into the night air with the softly falling snow; looking ahead, notice a small white flame flickering, and watch it as it expands to fill your vision and then gently fades as you slowly open your eyes. Allow yourself a little time to come into the present moment, gently rise, and go and blow out the candle.

Putting the Lessons of Goddesses into Practice

Considering the pros and cons of a confrontation can be of great benefit. Investors take a systematic approach when deciding where to put their money by weighing the risk against the payoff. So, when you know there is trouble ahead, a cost-benefit analysis can help you determine if it is worth the fight: ask yourself if the costs outweigh the benefits. If the costs are too high, it is better not to engage in the fight and just move on. But this does not mean that you must avoid all battles where the risks are high; indeed, sometimes you will fight on a matter of principle alone. The benefits of taking up a fight or seeking redemption do not have to be monetary; our moral judgement can come into play to prevent situations repeating themselves or to protect yourself or others, or to uphold rights. Each case is different, so it is beneficial to weigh the costs and benefits before deciding what to do.

Try to avoid the concept of having to "beat" or "crush" the person you are in conflict with, as this triggers a scarcity mindset: the idea that there must be a winner and a loser, or someone who's right and someone who's wrong. You will be limited emotionally and creatively. Remember, there are many possibilities to move forward or resolve things, which can only come from a mindset open to abundance. By focusing on how to resolve the situation, you will find emotions such as positivity, love, and optimism are fed into it. Remember, the battle isn't against your opponent, but against the conflict. For example, if you are angry, frustrated, or upset with your partner, avoid stoking the fire by being passive-aggressive; try talking to them to overcome or accept your differences so you can both achieve your goals together.

Having an open discussion can eliminate shutting down what both parties want, and it allows us to demonstrate respect for the other person's views, even if they are different from yours. Thoughts need to be aired and, if possible, look toward the best outcome for both parties. Tips for this type of conflict resolution include sharing your opinions; seeking to understand differing views; considering all ideas as being equally valid; allowing both sides to ask questions to gain a better understanding; being supportive to each other in the process by acknowledging what you hear; and working together to find the best solution for both parties.

It can be hard to not let emotions run high and say or do things you don't mean or will regret. Deep-seated grievances can surface, and you may feel like attacking the person, even though you know it will not end well, nor will it deliver the outcome that is needed. So having an exit strategy is essential. If you had all the time and money and emotional resilience in the world, perhaps you would be the victor in any situation. But we are not without our limits or without a conscience. Many people have suffered trying to resolve a problem or win a fight with either no answer or no end. If you cannot make any progress despite all your best efforts, then knowing when to cut your losses and move on or agree to disagree will be the best resolution for you. Remember that knowing when to let go, to move on, is a powerful weapon. But this can be easier said than done; it can be hard to mentally let go.

You may feel sad, angry, disappointed, or aggrieved, so it can help to get to the root causes of the issue. This can often unearth the best way to resolve it. Doing this can be a battle in itself; sometimes, we are afraid to uncover what lies beneath, to dig up the past, or to have to face our own demons. But you need not be alone in this undertaking. The creative energy that flows within you can also provide access to finding a way forward, to overcoming the obstacles that hold you in this confrontational state.

Hopefully, you will see the merit in picking your battles wisely. When it does come to taking one on, the energies of Maman Brigitte or Skadi will give you the strength, determination, courage, and patience to see it through for the best possible outcome for all;

one that is just and fair and moves you along on your path rather than hiding you in the past or drowning you in a sea of destructive emotions. There is no need for you to do that, to be the victim time and time again. The arguments, fights, and conflict we face need not harm even if it is not seen or felt in the immediate future. And this outcome is very heavily influenced by how we confront and deal with those situations.

Picking Your Battles, Resolution Tips

Author and mentor C. JoyBell C. wrote, "Pick your battles wisely because life is too short to spend it at war. Fight only the most, most, most important ones, let the rest go."[6] However, not all conflict can or should be avoided, so it is best to be prepared; that means understanding why we get into them, coping with them, and ultimately getting something productive from the outcome. It is all a matter of balance, of ensuring the ebb and flow, and when that is thrown out of kilter or is blocked, then something dramatic can ensue in an attempt the correct the imbalance. Make yourself familiar with all the tools or "weapons" at your disposal; the drive and courage of Maman Brigitte, the steely determination and emotional control of Skadi, your own communication skills, and your resolve to see it through. Employ them all, and you can face the future with far more room for optimism than doubt, and remember...

6   C. JoyBell C., *Vade Mecum.*

You will not always agree with others, hold the same views, or even see things in the same light. However, when things are taken further, and we argue, fight, bully, or force others against their will, it can land us in an exhausting and bloody battleground.

Prevention is better than cure; however, if circumstances are such that you cannot stop what is to happen, then being able to cope in that situation is a powerful weapon.

Engaging the directions has at its heart the purpose of restoring balance. This can be done by calling in a direction that offers you the qualities you lack, or a direction that enhances specific attributes, or both.

Becoming familiar with all the north and south aspects when picking our battles is ultimately about being equipped to engage productively and for the best outcome.

The north is the place of knowledge, reflection, patience, and learning, where the ancestors await. The journey to this direction manifests all that it holds for you and what you can access when there.

The south is the place of action, of putting knowledge into practice, the place of birthing energy, and living in full colour, where the healers dwell. The journey to this direction manifests all that it holds for you and what you can create when there.

When you need to get in amongst the action in the battle with conviction and passion, then Maman Brigitte holds an energy that enables you to do just that and heal from it.

When understood and applied holistically, redemption is a way of saving ourselves from further harm, or greater conflict, by helping us understand a contrasting situation or point of view rather than just apportioning blame. If we only seek to blame, we run the risk of repeating the same confrontational patterns again.

Most people struggle to contain their emotions when pushed into a corner and releasing them is often a natural defence mechanism that sometimes works well and sometimes can end in disaster. The goddess Skadi calls on you in these circumstances to think with a clear head rather than act with a fiery heart.

Knowing exactly how to navigate through difficulty with minimal or no harm done is a lifelong lesson. Still, much can be learned even now to avoid many unnecessary conflicts in life.

Our traditional idea of atoning for something is all too often laced with religious overtones of guilt that can invariably feel like a punishment for things in our past. But by seeing that atonement is just another way of keeping things in check, especially through difficult times, it acts as a shield to prevent us from irrevocable harm, either to ourselves or to others.

Confrontations do not come from nothing; there is always a trigger. And whether the trigger is fear-based or not, when we have to engage in conflict, there will always be a way to resolve it without having to "defeat" or "destroy" either or both parties involved.

It is not just about living to fight another day but, far more importantly, about finding ways of living that minimise the opportunities for confrontations to arise in the future.

CHAPTER 9

Death Becomes You

Nothing ever stays the same, and even the most well-prepared individuals can get caught short. Despite all our best efforts to keep things as they are, change will come. And for the vast majority of people, the change we fear most is a "death." By death, I am referring to the point at which all things come to an end; relationships, career, lifestyle, a dream, and yes, the loss of a loved one. In goddess terms, we look at death as an ending to old ways, old beliefs, relationships, stages of life, habits, and actions that no longer serve you or a community. Death in all its guises brings with it radical change; this can manifest in the way you live, your outlook, and fundamental behaviour often stemming from fear. The goddess energies that draw near now command both respect and reverence, their power fed by the soil and skies of Africa and South America. Their presence, at first glance, instils fear of the unknown, of death itself.

Still, in resolving to work with these aspects of our lives and ourselves, they provide an incredible opportunity to rebuild anew.

What we have done to this point, what we believe in, and the life we have built for ourselves could be so quickly taken away, we could be removed from it all and all we love. When we come to this point along our journey, we ask ourselves why and for what purpose? Perhaps we are being asked to give up our ego attachments to being "right" and to move into new realms of possibility. In the face of death in the form of fundamental change, who we are, what we stand for, comes into stark relief. We become aware that the harmony in life is shifting, we feel weighed down, and often, darkness prevails. These "initiatory deaths" occur most often during the middle years of life, often when we think we have finally "made our mark" and feel sure of ourselves, our opinions, beliefs, and identity. Your ego's strength is calling out to the world to be noticed for the unique and worthwhile being you have become. But you are not just your ego, and so often, at this time, a death can occur that shakes you to your core and makes you question yourself as if you were back in your early youth with so many fears and uncertainties.

Intuitively we know that great change, when it comes, is usually out of necessity, but there is still that voice in our heads that fears the change and tries to convince us that it is going to be the death of us and all we know; it can only be a bad thing. You may fall into that place of fear to avoid the "unknown" or to avoid the fact that the change required to really transform your situation may require effort, going beyond your comfort zone doing things you have put off. Your mind might be processing the change or the need to let go of things as a threat to you in a very physical sense, that you will lose who you are or all that you have. It is core to our survival to fight or resist anything that we perceive as a threat.

But you are more than just the body through which you experience your life. And this is often what holds us back; the limits of our physical vessel and the potential of our energetic, creative source or what we would call our soul or spirit. It is enough to remember, to believe, how expansive you really are, that there is much more in this world that is working with you rather than against you. An end to those things that are not helping you as a person or your experience of this life can be invited at earlier or advanced ages through clear intention and practices, like rites of passage, so long as you are emotionally developed enough to allow death (transformation) to occur.

When you sense this type of transformation coming on, this feeling of things slipping away, of having to surrender to situations that feel like they are going against our desires, you may well fear it because a genuine part of you knows that an end is coming to something you once valued or held dear. You will feel an urgency to hold on because of what "might" lie ahead. But you will realise that holding on at any level will cause discomfort, pain, and hardship. The goddess energy that calls to you in those times is the strength to go with the "unravelling." In the same way, when a car spins on an icy surface, the right thing to do is to turn into the spin, even though you want to fight against it. When faced with such a situation, a great change, a loss, or even what some refer to as a "dark night of the soul," remember that something new, even better, requires this moment, this process, to be born. You can also facilitate this process by opening up to the realities of death at all levels and so invite into your life those experiences, people, events, goddess guides, and other allies that will best assist your transition. Willingness to be responsible and accountable is your best ally.

This willingness starts by asking yourself, "What is there in my life that needs to die (old patterns of believing, thinking, reacting)? What do I want to release? What ways of being in the world no longer serve the people I am close to, or me? Do I play the victim or resort to anger too quickly? Do I fail to see alternatives? What really matters to me?" Confronting life-altering change, finding your feet in life again, often comes down to aligning yourself with natural energies and becoming aware of what is going on.

Remember the feelings of anxiety when you break a habit, end a relationship, give up a job, or change any "known" and familiar aspect of our lives? What you are feeling is freed-up energy. It needs to be redirected, or it is consumed in non-serving pursuits like worrying about the unknown. When you become willing to face this type of death, of release or letting go, less of your life is dictated by past personal history and is now directed by your own creative or spiritual growth. In other words, the more you learn to bend with the wind, the less likely you are to break, for the winds of change can be mighty indeed.

Engaging with Winds of Change

When it comes to natural forces of destruction in nature, those related to the power of wind rate very highly. Whether in the form of actual storms, hurricanes, tornadoes, or by way of fueling blizzards, stirring up rough seas, or fanning fires of epic proportions, the wind, this potentially most violent aspect of the element of air, has few equals. But like all the elements, it exists in other ways that balance out the chaos and disruption. It is a source of green energy, crucial to our weather systems and therefore our very existence, and there really is no more exhilarating feeling than "blowing out the cobwebs," so to speak, when out on a walk on a windy day. And there are few things as valuable as breathing exercises to calm the mind and relax the body.

The lessons the "wind" teaches are ingrained in folklore, like the three little pigs' story and the importance of building solid foundations. As a force for revelation, the wind can easily blow down or blow away anything pretentious or false, highlighting weakness or revealing the truth. It is not an element you need to shy away from or ward against, but learn to work with, embrace as a tool for helping you clear a path, see the actual options available, and the things in your life that will weather the storm.

The most common way in which we all engage with air is by breathing. But too often, this is compromised at the very time when we need it most when we are under pressure or feel attacked. In many spiritual practices, breathwork is very important. Martial artists understand that their ability to breathe fully and completely, especially when threatened by an opponent, is key to their success. When my present husband taught Tai Chi, new, overly eager students would occasionally ask him how soon the fighting techniques would be introduced. His reply would always be, "You need to learn to breathe properly first." By breathing consciously, you "still the mind" and your emotions, take more oxygen in, and prepare your body to enter into a deeply relaxed state in which you can more easily connect with your creative energy.

An elder of the Re-birthing movement, Leonard Orr, teaches an essential breathing exercise that you can practice whenever you feel overloaded, be it at work or home or in a social situation.[7] You can do this either sitting, lying down, or walking. You can close your eyes or keep them open, especially if you are using this breathing method to relax whilst on the move. Take a full but natural-length breath in through your nose and exhale through your nose. Repeat this natural and shallow breath two more times. Then, on the fourth breath, inhale more fully, taking more air in through your nose for longer. Then on the exhale, release your breath fully and completely, letting your body completely relax during the exhaling process. Repeat this pattern of three natural, short breaths and one long, deep breath at least four times (or longer if you wish). It is not a coincidence that this type of breathing exercise resembles a more passive version of the way in which women are taught to manage their breathing in labour.

---

7   Leonard Orr, *Breaking the Death Habit: The Science of Everlasting Life*, (North Atlantic Books, 1998).

As you began to breathe more consciously, you will open up to yourself and your world more fully. You are capable of instigating and coping with fundamental change. You are filled with potential and have access to a neverending source of creative energy. Like the blustering winds that uproot, throw everything in the air, and totally change the landscape from time to time, when we have the tools and the confidence, we can cope no matter how much it may feel like it is the death of us. And there is one goddess who encaptures all this and whose energy, be it chaotic or cathartic, is guaranteed to whip up a storm.

Deliverer of Disruption, Bringer of Storms

Thunder, lightning, tornadoes, blustering winds, hurricanes, and storms of magnitude are all types of natural disruptive forces closely associated with one of Africa's most potent orishas or goddesses, the whirlwind that is Oya. If you have ever been at the mercy of this type of weather, then you will understand how unsettling it can feel. A storm surge can wipe out an entire village, levelling buildings, clearing fields, uprooting trees, and so on, leaving a totally devastated and transformed landscape in a short space of time. This energy or force manifested into the goddess is the epitome of rapid change within, at once destroying what we are familiar with and forcing us to start anew. But rapid change aids us in both inner and outer transformation. In this regard, Oya is the wind in our sails, propelling us forward. Hers is a power that can be harnessed to sweep all injustice, deceit, and dishonesty from your path. Oya is considered the patron of feminine leadership, and in that capacity, she protects all who participate in witchcraft, childbirth, and other traditionally female-dominated pursuits.

◎ HAILING THE DIVINE FEMININE INVOCATION

When the Divine Feminine energy draws near, you are more likely to feel it than see it. The sensation can range from the mild unease of "butterflies in the stomach" to being engulfed in total devastation. A loss of clarity or direction, a sense of confusion, or feeling bereft of all control may overcome you. The noise in your head can be unbearable, and you might be sensitive to the slightest pin-dropping. But as with all the goddess energy that we encounter in life, it is worth remembering that there will be a reason. Do not be dissuaded, for this energy can be the most potent ally, holding you in the eye of the storm and getting you through it to the other side.

YOU WILL NEED:

* A quiet space, where you can be seated at a table undisturbed for twenty to thirty minutes

* Pen and paper

* A small handheld bell for clearing

* Three candles: orange (or gold) for direction, black for protection, and purple for intuition

* Sandalwood essential oil

* An offering to the Divine Feminine, small enough to hold in one hand and place on your focal point; this could be any red gemstone, any object in the shape of an egg, or any object made of copper

Begin by preparing the space; do this by ringing the bell over the table and where you will be seated, then place the bell down on the floor out of harm's way. Create a triangular space using the candles on the table with the orange candle at the top, the black candle to the left, and the purple candle to the right. Finally, place your offering in the middle of the triangle and place a drop or two of sandalwood oil on it. Just take a moment now to consider some of the changes you want to make—it might just be one or a few—and write them down, leaving enough space between for the goddess's inspiration which you will tap into shortly.

Next, you need to light all three candles starting with the black one, then orange, and then purple and set your intention; you can do this aloud or in your head but simply say, *I call upon the goddess to share her energy with me today, for the change to come. Blessed be.* So now we go about invoking her energy in its three primary forms. Begin by focusing on the black candle and say, *Hail Deliverer of Disruption, protect me with your energy, as the ground shakes beneath my feet, and my life is swept up in the challenges I must now be prepared to meet.* Turn your attention next to the orange candle and say, *Hail Warrior of Winds, blow through me with your energy, so all I was, I am, and am yet to be, are no longer bound together, but set free.* Turn your attention now to the purple candle and say, *Hail Bringer of Change, guide me with your energy, to only pick up the pieces that matter to me, to reshape and reform as it should now be.*

When you feel ready, or sense the goddess's presence, refer to your notes and reveal them one at a time to her (you can do this aloud or in your head). Focus on the positive aspects of these changes, then close your eyes and allow the messages to come back to you from the goddess. Consider the action you will need to take, to whom you might need to speak, when the changes might be achievable—in a day or two, a week, or by this time next year, for example. Always be honest and realistic. Take the time to visualise yourself carrying out the changes, see yourself doing this successfully, even navigating any pitfalls or coming up with good reasons for those who might question your choices. Then when you are ready, open your eyes and take the piece of paper, fold it three times and hold it in both hands and say, *I pledge to the goddess to honour my changes and carry them out in the time I have chosen to the best of my ability, blessed be.*

Finally, focus on the offering in the middle and say, *Hail goddess, with this offering I give thanks for your protection, guidance, and transformation, to weather the storm that is about to visit me, blessed be.* Allow a minute or two for quiet contemplation, then blow out the candles. Your offering and paper should be placed somewhere safe, like your focal point or in a place of meaning to you, in the knowledge that through it, you can call on the Divine Feminine energy whenever you feel the need or just wish to be in that energetic presence. If you want a boost while making your changes, or want to make more, use this ritual again to engage this powerful energy. Put the candles and smudging tools away and go about your day.

Taking in the Lessons of Oya's myths

Like the one for Hekate, the above invocation is primarily about a transfer of the goddess energy, in this case harnessing it in your offering and making actual plans to change aspects of your life for the better. As has been explained, Oya's lessons are most often experienced as a force of nature; however, some people may actually "see" her manifest before them. She may appear one of two ways, depending on whether you are embracing or resisting the changes. Resistance brings a vision of the "warrior woman." Her jet-black skin, shining like armour. Her hair wild and her eyes white and glowing. She is bejewelled in silver from top to toe, scantily clad and with a weapon in one hand, usually a staff or spear and either lightning or fire pulsating in her other hand. This is Oya in full force, as the storm, as the destruction, the energy of upheaval and chaos. Brace yourself, for this is an indicator that the changes are imminent or have just begun. Or you may encounter the other aspect of Oya, as "the protector," appearing with an arm outstretched, her hand beckoning to you, her staff dormant in her other hand. Her curvaceous figure now fully clothed. Her eyes are no longer glowing white but dark, soulful, and intense. When this version of Oya appears, it is a reminder that you can deal with what is happening, you are in the eye of the storm, catching your breath, making plans, and soon the changes will be over, and the new way ahead will be revealed to you.

My experiences with these lessons have been very much by way of sensing emotional turmoil rather than actually seeing a goddess. When my best friend died, I had to identify the body. It was not a pleasant affair; I was young, and his death was a shock that I really was not prepared for. When I saw his body in the morgue, my initial instinct was to take it home with me; it was so cold to the touch and hard that, in my grief, I thought by bringing it home and making it warm, I could bring my friend some comfort, wherever he was. But my father reminded me that it was not my friend who lay there; it was just a body that my best friend once occupied. It was not until a couple of months later, in the process of releasing my friend's ashes in a very sacred place, that I actually experienced him leave and felt the peace my best friend had finally found.

In that moment, the part of me that had died in the hospital morgue was reborn again among some ancient castle ruins, on a cliff edge, with a blustering wind smacking my cheeks as I faced out to sea and wished the person who was once my whole future safe passage. You see, we are conditioned to believe that all deaths of our loved ones are tragic. But in all of them, no matter how painful for those left behind, a passing offers opportunity. Something beautiful

or purposeful can occur when those left living are open to the possibilities of making the most of their lives, of greater appreciation,
whether it is in little ways or in big, bold, radical changes. For some
people, it is really like getting their hands dirty and unearthing a
new way of living.

Digging in the Dirt

We have already touched on the great importance the element of
earth plays in our lives, in all life. Its ability to transform energy,
store energy, and release it. The ability the earth has to bury and
contain gases. These minerals should remain safe underground, out
of harm's way, as well as the ability to nurture the resources we need
just below the surface until we cultivate them. When referring to
getting our hands dirty emotionally and spiritually, to unearth what
must come to the surface, it is about exploring the things, experiences, actions, and words that we have buried within. Just like the
way in which earth retains things that should never be exploited, so
too you will have had experiences that you have dealt with, come to
terms with, that are best left within.

But these will be few compared to those experiences that are
trapped just below the surface, which can only be resolved when
you choose to do so. Some of these experiences may include childhood trauma, abuse (both as a victim or perpetrator), loss of a loved
one, self-worth issues, mental health issues, life-changing events,
broken relationships, or money worries, to name a few. All of these
experiences can eat at you, kill off a tiny part of you, and continue

to consume your energy while they remain just below the surface. You will know what they are because they will give you an uneasy feeling in the pit of your stomach or weigh heavy on the heart at the slightest thought of them.

Holding all that toxic energy at bay is exhausting, mentally and physically; people become anxious, struggle to sleep, eat, have no motivation to exercise, or over-exercise. You feel you are not living but existing; you are not thriving but surviving. It is time to face the fear that confronting what you have buried will bring the world around you to an end. But digging in your own dirt is more about transforming something that feels like an ending into a new beginning, making way for something better to grow in the place where you have allowed something to stagnate or fester. It takes a lot of courage to address these experiences, even to openly acknowledge their existence or the impact they have on you. Perhaps just the thought of doing this is too much.

But you are not alone; most people struggle with bad experiences that have been swept under the carpet, unresolved. It is sadly a consequence of the modern way of life where we have lost so much of our connection with our natural environment. We have muted our intuitive understanding of the natural cycles and our rites of passage, favouring a far more detached, materialistic, consumer-based existence. Our traditional, ancient rites of passage are ceremonies that mark the crucial stages in life, like birth, puberty, marriage, and death. It is time to get back to your roots, to the root of what ails you so severely, time to get your hands dirty and immerse yourself in the middle of it. What follows is an adaptation of a traditional rite of passage that you can undertake to prepare yourself for revelation, healing, and transformation.

◎ BURIED IN EARTH EXERCISE

To be "buried in earth" is a powerful shamanic ritual still practised worldwide to promote emotional healing, reconnection, and transformation. When undertaken in its most authentic form, the initiate will dig their own grave in which they will spend from several hours up to an entire night in darkness and silence. They are encased in the earth, breathing only through a straw-like tube, surrendering themselves to the process and the earth's embrace. This is an intense experience that very few people get to encounter these days. It is not something you can undertake alone either, but if you are drawn to deep communion with nature and are prepared to open yourself to being with your innermost thoughts and feelings, then there is a way you can undergo a version of this ritual. This version still enables you to recover your inner power and forge a more harmonious relationship with yourself by releasing internal resistance, negative thought patterns, and negative energies that prevent you from moving forward with your life. It helps to give you space and energy to come to terms with the issues you have pushed aside or hidden. Returning to nature in this way reconnects the heart and soul with your journey, especially when you have suffered significant loss or been embroiled in a chaotic way of life.

YOU WILL NEED:

* A quiet space in nature, where you will not be disturbed for an hour or two

* A sleeping bag, something to rest your head on and enough blankets to cover yourself from top to toe, at least two layers

In preparation, it is worth picking your spot outside in advance; you will be spending a bit of time there and need to be comfortable. The space might need to be prepared by clearing away loose vegetation, stones, or rocks, giving you enough space to lie down in comfort. Pick a day when it is overcast; you want a feeling of darkness within your sleeping bag and beneath your blankets. Once you have chosen and prepared your space, then lie down inside your sleeping bag, take the blankets, and cover yourself from feet to face, allowing a gap to breathe. Now close your eyes. Starting at your feet, feel the sensation of the earth beneath you. Then pay attention to the warmth and weight of the sleeping bag and blankets around you. Think of the weight like a "hug," using your imagination to see yourself covered in earth, being hugged by the earth, held in the soil. Allow that sensation and visualisation to travel up along your body, your legs feeling encased, then your pelvis, hips, and torso, feeling the weight and warmth.

Notice the feeling of your head on the cushion and imagine that too as a warm sort of soil. And finally, your face is under the "earth." It is warm and comforting and quiet.

Now, with eyes still closed, use the Leonard Orr basic breathing technique. Take a full but natural-length breath in through your nose and exhale through your nose. Repeat this natural and shallow breath two more times. Then, on the fourth breath, inhale more fully, taking more air in through your nose for a longer time. On the exhale, release your breath fully and completely, letting your body completely relax during the exhaling process. Repeat this pattern of three natural, short breaths and one long, deep breath for the next fifteen minutes. Return your breathing to your usual way while allowing yourself to sink under the weight of the blankets and your mind to empty of your daily concerns; just relax into the sensations of the natural world around you.

Imagine now, with every out-breath, all worries and concerns leaking out of every pore in your body being absorbed by the earth. They are carried away in the roots of the flowers, plants, trees, and grasses, taken up by the stems, transformed into pure neutral energy to feed the petals, leaves, and blades of grass. On the in-breath, imagine the earth squeezing you a little, not too much but enough to notice, gently encouraging your negative energy to come to the surface and be absorbed. Continue with this gentle releasing for as long as you feel comfortable. Then gradually open your eyes and peel away the layers of blankets and rise up out of your sleeping bag. Give thanks, tidy up the space, and go about your day.

The exercise you have just experienced is all about allowing your mental and physical self to "die" to its everyday demands and be "held" in the transformative power of earth, to reconnect with the space that held you in the womb, where it was warm, dark, and quiet. All that you were required to do was just to be. And when you are held in the earth, all that is asked of you is just to be yourself, not a reason or a solution, just you, breathing and relaxing and recovering, letting the earth work its magic. The next goddess takes the magical powers of earth to another level; she is a most proactive force of goddess energy, doing all she can to go to extreme lengths to ensure that the cycle of life is maintained.

Eater of Sin, Purifier of Souls

In Aztec mythology, Tlazolteotl is an earth goddess whose sphere of influence is broader and more unusual than other goddesses of the earth and fertility. Her duties are three-fold: to encourage "sin" to the surface, to eat the sin, and then to purify the soul. According to Aztec belief, Tlazolteotl is known to inspire latent immoral behaviour in people, causing them to engage in illicit sexual acts, and then afflicting disease upon them. The uncleanliness was seen as both a physical and moral blight and was said to be cleansed by a steam bath or a rite of purification. It is worth noting that adultery was punishable by death in Aztec society, so it was a great relief to the offender that they could escape this fate by confessing their sins to the great goddess.

But this confession could only be heard once in a lifetime by Tlazolteotl, so people would save it for when it was really needed or as a last resort. Tlazolteotl's name is derived from the Nahuatl word for rubbish or waste, making her the goddess of the black, fertile earth, the fecund earth that gains its energy from death, and in turn, feeds life. She turns all garbage, or excrement, physical and metaphysical, into fertile life by eating it. This aspect of Tlazolteotl is depicted in images of her with a blackened mouth.

This "filth" is seen as a metaphor for wrongdoing or sin. Though all filth is considered Tlazolteotl's domain, she always completes the circle by purifying immoral behaviour. Those that were close to death would be encouraged to confess their sins to her; she would then "eat" these bad deeds, thus purifying the individual, cleansing their bodies, minds, and souls, and in so doing preparing them for the afterlife. These days "sin-eating" is understood as a form of ritual most commonly associated with Welsh culture, but "sin-eaters" appear in many different cultures and throughout folklore worldwide. A "sin-eater" is a person who consumes a ritual meal to spiritually take on the sins of a deceased person. As a consequence, these people carry the sins of all people whose sins they had eaten. In Upper Bavaria, Germany, sin-eating still survives; a "corpse cake" rests on the chest of the dead before it is consumed by the closest relative. Along the Balkan peninsula, family members of the deceased eat a small bread image of their dead relative, and "burial-cakes" are still made in parts of rural

England as a relic of sin-eating. It has also been depicted in films such as *The Green Mile* and in "The Gift" episode of the TV series *The X-Files*.

Tlazolteotl executed her responsibilities and fulfilled her role in the confession of wrongdoing through her priests. The ritual required to obtain her pardon was complicated. First, the priest would consult the heavens, books, and calendars to decide the best day to hear the confession. On that day, the penitent would strip naked and humbly and honestly confess their sins. The priest would then prescribe a fast to purify the body, and the penitent then chooses their sacrifice. After the sacrifice was made, the penitent spent the night praying in the temple of Tlazolteotl, lying naked on black paper on the floor.

The following morning the ritual would end when the penitent woke up reborn and purified, having had their sins consumed by the goddess. In tribute, Tlazolteotl was one of the primary Aztec deities celebrated during the harvest season. The ceremonies included ritual cleaning, sweeping, and repairing, as well as the casting of corn seed, dances, and military ceremonies to preside over purification. So, through her processes and rituals, Tlazolteotl helped create harmony in communities. She is the provoker and the pardoner, and it was believed that without her, the cycle of death and life would be broken, and we would cease to exist.

No one goes through life without making mistakes, and most of us, at some point, will engage in "wrongdoing" of one kind or another. Few people will break the law, but our words and deeds carry immense power, and sometimes we do harm with them. And most people do not feel at ease when they cause such harm. This is the most common type of "dis-ease" to receive help from the goddess's energy when we are genuinely open to it. We no longer consult spiritual or religious leaders for the more severe crimes and spend time making sacrifices at temples. Today we have the justice system: fines, probation, incarceration, and in some countries, capital punishment. In modern religion, we see echos of Tlazolteotl's influence via confession, and people praying to Mother Mary; even the sacrifice of Christ on the cross can be seen as an extreme act of one person taking on the sins of all people to make anew. But this is not why you would engage with the goddess's energy now.

◎ Feeding the Earth Ritual

What follows is a ritual to help you face any "dis-ease" within, acknowledge it, and then let it "die" to Tlazolteotl so that you have the energy and both head and heart space to create something better, or more productive, or just feel better about yourself and where you are on your journey.

You will need:

* A quiet space outside in nature where you will be undisturbed for fifteen to twenty minutes

* Tools to "clear" or cleanse the space, ideally a bell or rattle

> * A "food" offering, to consist of a slice of stale
> (not mouldy) brown bread, a handful of
> sunflower seeds, and a raw egg

Once you have found your "sacred space," the place where you can practise this ritual without being disturbed, you need to energetically "clear" the space. Do this by taking your bell or rattle and proceed by cleansing the four directions (full details of this can be found in Chapter 1 as part of "Creating a Simple Focal Point"). When you are done, put your cleansing tools to one side and, holding the seeds in your dominant hand, stand in the middle of your space, facing the direction most comfortable to you, and call in Tlazolteotl by saying, *Hail Revealer of Sin, I call to you to bring to the surface the ills and wrongdoings that must come to light, as I now throw these seeds upon the earth for you to expose what festered inside with all your might.* With that, scatter the seeds over the ground all around you. Then take the slice of bread and, standing in the middle of the space, hold it to your chest and say, *Hail Eater of Sin, I ask of you now to harness in this offering what can no longer be, take it inside you to cleanse and transform and make space within me.*

With that, break up the slice into smaller pieces and scatter it over the ground around you. Finally, take the egg in your dominant hand, hold it against your belly and say, *Hail Purifier of Souls, I ask of you now to impregnate this offering with potential and grace, make from it something positive and new, so the old energy has no longer a place.* With that, break the egg open on the ground in front of you. Give thanks by saying *Hail Tlazolteotl, I thank you for your presence as I leave my offerings to feed the earth, in the same way that you have enriched me, by taking what was spent and spoilt and setting it free. Blessed be.* Finally, collect your belongings, leaving all the "offerings" for the birds and the bees, the earth and the trees, and go about your day.

It may be that you get a real sense of relief or release when doing this ritual for the first time. You may not hear or see or sense the goddess in person, but she will be there in the soil on the ground, the leaves on the trees, the petals on flowers, or the creatures crawling below the surface. She will be in the wind, she will hear and see, and she will feed. Suppose you do encounter Tlazolteotl in her most generic personification. In that case, you will be most likely struck by the trademark blackened mouth, her large headdress, and naked torso, usually covered in earth. She is a goddess or action rather than words, so she will say little but might gesture for you to "feed" her. This ritual is not to be used like a confessional, i.e. to excuse immoral or destructive behaviour. It can then be absorbed by the goddess; if we were all doing that, the goddess would soon become overwhelmed and literally drown in our filth. It is better to treat it more like a "spring clean" of the body, mind, and soul. Perhaps perform it once a year, or like a rite of passage at the most poignant times in life.

Times of Death and Transformation

The cycle of death and rebirth, of giving up the old to create or embrace the new, is by no means a rare event that occurs but a few times in life; it happens all the time. Nature is the personification of that cycle; we human beings are the only ones who actively fight against it, putting ourselves under constant pressure to stay young, to cling to long-held ideas and beliefs even if they are not our own or we no longer believe them in our hearts. We hoard material things, consume more than we need or, in some cases, more than we could ever use. We cling on to old ways of doing something out of greed or laziness or fear; look at how we get our energy, for example. And by refusing to let some of these things "die," we prevent better things and better ways of living to take hold, and in the process, we make ourselves ill-at-ease, we breed dis-ease within ourselves and our environment at large. If we practice again celebrating death and transformation, we can heal and move past fears and our own dis-ease in the face of change.

One excellent way this can be done is by celebrating key times in our seasons; these holidays already exist, but we have forgotten how to celebrate them with sincerity and authenticity, so the significance and power of them is lost. I invite you now to reclaim just two of these holidays and celebrate them as intended so that you can help keep the cycle of death and rebirth to continue more smoothly, at least in your life. The first of these is the Celtic festival of Samhain (pronounced "sow-en"), which, unlike its commercial incarnation

Halloween, has nothing to do with tricks or treats, superhero, zombie, or scary costumes, or sinister practices and scaring people. It marks the end of autumn and the beginning of winter. To the Celtic people of Europe, winter was not seen as the beginning of the end of the year but rather the beginning of the New Year.

Everything was now being conceived, growing within, preparing itself for spring; the dark months are the beginning. Samhain was the day of honouring those who had passed over when the veil between the worlds of the living and the dead was at its thinnest. This was when communication between these worlds was at its strongest, and the living could ask the ancestors for assistance or advice. The ancestors were lovingly remembered; often, a place was left for them at the dinner table; sometimes, this place was set aside for the Great Mother, the family's original ancestor or clan. Candles were lit in the windows to help the ancestors find their way home for the celebration or to invite in any "lost soul" as a mark of respect and hospitality.

The women of these cultures would perform rituals to promote protection from harm and negativity, like lighting large fires on hilltops, thus projecting positive actions and outcome onto the future, like fertile soil, fruitful harvest, good health, and prosperity for the community. People would write down things they wanted to change, release, or get rid of on paper that would then be ceremonially burned, setting their intention for changing things for the better, called "the papers of regret."

Apples, harvested at this time, were considered a sacred and magical fruit because when cut crosswise, it reveals the five-pointed star at its core, a symbol of the goddess, of life, and immortality. Apples were buried at this time to feed those souls who are waiting to be reborn. Apple cider was also used not just as a drink but to feed the trees to honour the source of the fruits, a tradition known as "wassailing the trees." Cakes were baked with charms inserted that would hint at the lucky recipient's future; for example, a coin in your piece of cake would indicate good fortune, or a ring for marriage. All of these activities had one thing in common: the promise of new beginnings, no matter how dark or bleak the times are now.

The other festive time heralds these new beginnings. Ostara celebrates the time when the light of day and night are equal, with new signs of life and fertility, like budding shoots of green growth and blossoming flowers. It is the time when we emerge fully out of the sacred darkness into the bright, blessed light. The new ideas created during the dark resting times are birthed, and we literally spring into action. Adopted by Christianity, it is often grouped with Easter celebrations. These rituals were so important to ancient cultures that Christianity connected the traditional return of the celestial body, the sun, to the religious resurrection of the Son. This time is about your renewal, the birth of your new or changed life after a "death" of sorts. We feel more energised, so be encouraged to do what you really want to or need to, especially if it involves any physical or artistic activity. The time for thinking and planning is done; now it is the time for action.

The main thrust of this chapter, of this part of your journey, is to show you that an end of things in your life is not something to fear or fight, or to worry over to the point that it makes you ill, but rather that it is the most necessary thing for you to live better. Death as darkness is not a place without hope; it is the very place that hope can be conceived. These times in our lives when we feel at our lowest ebb, at rock bottom, are, in fact, the perfect times to really assess what is wrong and begin to turn things around when we are able to recognise them as such. This is not to say that losing a person you love, even a child, will not feel genuinely devasting, and you may question why carry on at all … but to add to that loss by giving up on your life, on those still living who love you, would be the most incomprehensible tragedy. To rise from such a dark time and be a positive influence in life, to find joy and happiness again, is the best gift and best use of your creative power, and above all the best way to transform your feelings of loss into love.

Death Becomes You, Resolution Tips

It is often said that the darkest hour is before the dawn. When you are at your wits' end, when you face the prospects of a void instead of a life due to loss, heartache, or hardship beyond your control, it takes confidence and courage to ride it out until you see the light of day. But be assured for as long as you draw breath, there will be a way forward. The idea of death is necessary to continue your journey, even if, at first, it feels uncomfortable or impossible. Our "deaths" while we are alive are an opportunity to release beliefs, change our minds, get out of bad relationships, improve our character, and learn to cope with all that life has to offer. Embrace these deaths as they are an indicator that positive transformation is waiting for you, and remember:

> Begin your cycle by being honest with yourself. Ask the essential questions of yourself, like who matters, am I in the right job, am I being heard, am I listening, am I in the right relationship, do I thrive where I live, do I know where I am at in life and where I want to go?

> The wind is instrumental in the distribution of weather patterns around the globe being maintained in such a way as to ensure the living conditions are right for us. Our ancestors understood this and revered this force of nature.

> For the soul, wind can be read as a destructive force or a force that helps blow things through for us. In coming to understand your connection with this element as part of the cycle of death and life, endings and beginnings, you can learn to embrace it energetically rather than fear it.

> Learn and practise breathing well, albeit in everyday life, during meditation or visualisations, or as a tool to gather your thoughts or stop your heart from racing

when under stress. This has an immediate impact to put us in a better state to think and act more clearly.

The Divine Feminine teaches you that if you persevere, you do not win or lose in life but rather win or learn. Invoking this energy draws on some of the most powerful emotions we carry, so be sure this is the right time and place to do so. In times of real crisis, when fundamental changes in direction, behaviour, or way of life are required, the strength gained can be a force of great upheaval, so be prepared.

Digging in the dirt is about foraging around in your very being to root out what has to go and what must be nurtured or left as they are. The more you do this type of "home" or "house" work on yourself, the easier it becomes, and the better you understand yourself.

Being buried in earth, giving yourself up to nature in this way, allowing yourself to be open and vulnerable again, as you were in your mother's womb, can be very liberating and healing.

The goddess Tlazolteotl is a reminder that there are three parts to the process of death and rebirth within ourselves: allowing what troubles us to surface and be inspected; allowing that to be analysed and a plan made as to what to do; and then taking action to do it. She is also a reminder that we can cultivate within us the ability to be open, honest, courageous, practical, and believe in our convictions. This way, "death" becomes a process for a continued fruitful life, devoid of waste or regret.

"Feeding the Earth" gives something of ourselves up to the tremendous transformative network that is our environment to recycle. And in a small way, our food offerings help sustain that environment— better use of our energy than allowing it to fester and become hateful or fearful inside us to be used against others or ourselves destructively.

Samhain, being the time to remember the ancestors, to commune with them, is also a great time to ritually feed the earth, rejoice at what has gone before, and look forward to what is to come, to make plans and to take the time to rest a little so you have the energy and enthusiasm you will need when it's time to implement the changes to come, be they major or minor.

Ostara is all about taking up the opportunities now open to you from the decisions and actions taken to release and let go of what was holding you back, from the big and little deaths you experienced in order to make the space and save the energy for the new; use it well.

CHAPTER 10

Born-Again Creator

The natural world shows us what it is to live in balance and harmony, what effort that takes, and how we must always consider the bigger picture or rise from the ashes. Your existence is no different. But knowing or recognising that you have all this potential within is not the same as being able to freely apply it. How do you manifest better relationships, a more fulfilling career, a calmer, more balanced stance in life, or exercise greater control over your emotional responses to events in life? Practice. Remember, you come into being as one incredible vessel. You do not come into life being broken, or only half-made, as you might be led to believe. Much of what you will create or manifest, you can also let go of and share. In sharing our creations, in the sharing of our lives, and in the sharing of ourselves, we make all those who feel "lesser than" feel more complete. The ultimate goal of the creator, of any individual who truly lives, is to experience life completely, the ups and downs, and still be at one with it all.

All as One

Looking at this from the mystical belief in numbers, the number 1 comes to mind now, as the origin of all that you bring forth. We think of this number to mark all the "beginnings" that we make in life, like the first day of the month or the first day of a new job. Within divination systems like the tarot and the I Ching, the number 1 donates self-determination, self-sufficiency, assertion, and the ability to take the lead—all qualities you need to create all aspects of your life positively within work, relationships, and self-awareness. In the tarot, the Magician is card 1 of the major arcana. This is a creative powerhouse brimming with confidence and grand life plans. In the Upanishads, the Hindu sacred text, the belief is that universe was just one single being, but the desire to create and become a part of a greater whole brought forth all of the diversity that we know of in the universe.

Relating to a much older time, when stories tell of the continents of Atlantis and Lumeria, the inhabitants (some believe to be our very, very distant ancestors) were neither male nor female, but both. In my interview with the entertainer and author Shirley MacLaine for her book *Sage-ing While Age-ing*, she told me she felt the single biggest mistake those races made was to genetically "split" people to create a male and female version. She believed this has since created such immense division and inequality, which we are still trying to correct, many tens of thousands of years later. I thought this was a fascinating idea, and as a concept, it explained our need to fill voids and create to find the missing part of ourselves. Now, in the world that generations of humans have created and where women have birthed the people to fill it, change it, and be changed by it, you can take up the mantle to be the difference you want to see in this world. Time to meet the final goddess, the "one" to bring you full circle and remind you how capable you really are...

She Who Creates and Sustains

As has just been stated, the goddess you are about to meet takes your creative journey full circle, as she is the goddess who encompasses all and everything that we need to survive and thrive physically, emotionally, and spiritually. In Greek mythology, Gaia is the primordial mother goddess who governed the universe. In their creation myth, the Greeks refer to the primordial soup of the universe as Chaos, a void of darkness and confusion. And who else could fill this void better than Gaia, who, as the master creator, brought forth the starry heavens, in the shape of the sky god Uranus, and the Earth itself as we know it today: a place of incredibly diverse landscapes and abundant with life. She is often depicted as a buxom, motherly figure rising from and intertwined with the earth. In some mosaics, she is a full-figured woman, reclining on the land, clothed in green and surrounded by all manner of flora and fauna.

The goddess is considered to be the fundamental life force of the Earth as well as its creator. Her powers and abilities include geokinesis (the ability to psychically alter earth's texture, density, fluidity, and temperature as well as induce or prevent natural phenomena like sinkholes, mudslides, earthquakes, and volcanic eruptions); chlorokinesis (the ability to summon, control, and manipulate plants and vegetation); and deity creation, regeneration, and immortality. No surprise that Gaia is also believed by some to be the original deity behind the Oracle at Delphi. And depending on the source, it is said that she passed this duty on to Poseidon, Apollo, or Themis. But Gaia's story is not just one of immense creative power, but of the importance of nurturing our creations rather than destroying them. This is demonstrated in a part of Gaia's myth that talks of her offspring.

Gaia had many children, in batches, of different species. First came the Kyklopes, then the Hekatonkheires and then the Titans. Once the elder Kyklopes and Hekatoncheires were born, Ouranos, the father of the Titans, threw them into the deepest region of the world, where the gods locked up their enemies out of fear of being overthrown. Gaia was so aggrieved that she fashioned a sickle out of the hardest flint and gave it to Cronos, one of her Titan sons. He convinced four of his brothers to help kill their father to avenge his older siblings' banishment. Gaia later warned Cronos about his own son dethroning him, which led to Cronos swallowing all his offspring, bar one Zeus, who Gaia had convinced Cronos' wife Rhea to hide. When Zeus returned as an adult, he convinced his father to "spit out" his siblings, and together they overthrew Zeus. But sadly, Zeus had not learned the lesson of valuing rather than overthrowing.

When he became king and imprisoned the Titans, Gaia was enraged again by her grandson's actions, warning him that one day he too could be overthrown. Zeus went as far as eating his pregnant wife Metis, an act that ended up bringing about his daughter, the goddess of wisdom and warfare, Athena. Gaia is also believed by some to be the original deity behind the Oracle at Delphi, where it is said she was the source from which all the vapours producing divine inspiration arose, later passing this duty on to Apollo. In her role as the all-producing and all-nourishing mother, her worship was universal amongst the ancient Greeks. Temples were dedicated to her throughout ancient Greece: in Athens, Sparta, Delphi, Olympia, Bura, and Tegea, to name a few.

There are significant similarities between the role and veneration of Gaia in the past and the monastic religious followers' place on God today. Highly respected archaeologist and anthropologist Marija Gimbutas identified Gaia as a later form of a pre-Indo-European "Great Mother," who was venerated in Neolithic times.[8] She put forth the case that it was the worship of the goddess that came before the worship of the god, even going so far as to say that under goddess worship, times for humanity were more peaceful, respectful, and nourishing.

---

8 Marija Gimbutas, *The Civilization of the Goddess: The World of Old Europe* (San Francisco: Harper, 1991).

In 1997, scientist and environmentalist James Lovelock brought his "Gaia hypothesis" to the world, a hypothesis supported by renowned biologist Lynn Margulis. Lovelock's hypothesis proposes that living organisms and inorganic material are part of a system that shapes the Earth's biosphere and maintains the Earth as a fit environment for life. And in some Gaia theories, the earth itself is viewed as one community of organisms that self-regulates all its functions: a single, complex entity, a goddess that Gaia personifies globally, both in the very distant past and now.[9]

And here is the thing: you are Gaia-like; your body is energy manifested as flesh and blood maintained by vitamins, minerals etc. but fueled or motivated by your will, your emotions, your spiritual presence, your desire to be. Every minute of every day, just like Gaia, you create, nurture, and sustain life. And just like Gaia, you are influenced by and react according to others' actions, and by your environment.

◎ GAIA ATTUNEMENT EXERCISE

This exercise is about experiencing your presence in your natural environment, beyond your perception of yourself, beyond the ego. By releasing yourself from your feelings and thoughts, you open up the potential for communion with that which transcends your ego. We usually do this by turning inward, but there is a type of meditation called "attunement"

---

9   James Lovelock, *The Ages of Gaia: A Biography of Our Living Earth* (New York: W. W. Norton, 1995).

that encourages you to turn outward. Like other forms of meditation, during the attunement, you give yourself permission to be absorbed by something beyond the ego, but focus your awareness on becoming one with Gaia, the greater circle of all creation. In attunement, you start with self-attunement (sensing your body and its processes), and you focus outward until your expanded awareness reaches a sense of oneness with life that encompasses all there is.

YOU WILL NEED:

* A quiet space outdoors where you will be undisturbed for ten to fifteen minutes

Once you have selected your place in nature, make yourself comfortable, either sitting or lying down, to prepare for your attunement. Start this connection/attunement by closing your eyes and taking three deliberate, deep breaths in through the nose and out through the mouth. Breathe in to the count of three, hold to the count of three, and breathe out to the count of three. Allow the air to completely fill your lungs on each breath and allow all the air to leave your lungs on the breath out.

Next, whilst returning your breathing to be more regular, work your way up from your toes to your head, consciously relaxing any muscles that seem tight, so they rest easily. You may want to adjust the position you are sitting or lying in as you relax your muscles; feel free to do so to be most comfortable.

Feel and welcome the presence of the earth beneath you. Next, whilst continuing to breathe normally, open your eyes and begin by focusing on any object in your direct line of vision. While looking at that object, allow your vision to gradually expand, soften your focus, and include what is in your peripheral vision. As your focus softens, expand your awareness to include what is in the immediate environment beyond your peripheral vision.

Continue this expansion of your "vision" until it encompasses everything about you. All the shapes of nature blend into one all-encompassing picture of a single living entity, a three-dimensional image of life before your eyes which you are a part of too. At this point, you may feel a slight tingling in the pelvis at the base of your spine. This may spread through your body, like a low-frequency current of electricity, or a feeling of butterflies in your tummy, or even just a sensation of "bliss." However, do not be discouraged if you have difficulty at first, either focusing on something near or expanding your vision to go beyond it.

The important thing is to not get stuck on the natural object but to flow through it and allow it to carry you beyond yourself, like the spreading of the ripples of a pebble dropped into a pond. Some people may not be entirely at home in the natural realm and may find it challenging to allow Gaia to draw them beyond themselves. If you are one of those people, I urge you to keep trying; with practice, it will come. Even without getting the whole experience, participating in this attunement positively influences the body and mind and reconnects you to the most fundamental source of life itself.

Your Creation Story

All civilisations have creation myths or stories, like a collective dream, to explain how things began. These accounts have been described as the first stage in the psychic or emotional life of a civilisation; they reveal our real priorities and prejudices. As our images of creation explain how we came to be as a people, so do the things you create say a lot about who you are. When you believe yourself to be a little "Gaia" all on your own, yet still an integral part of all that makes up the single entity that we call life, you will see that in your world, you have millions of ways of expressing yourself through the life you create and lead. Remember, your world is full of opportunities, but sometimes you can get lost in the thoughts of what could be, rather than making those plans come to life and living them. And when you spend too much time in reflection, scrutinising what might happen, all the potential outcomes and all the risk, you can get bogged down in the negativities. And that is what your manifestations will be governed by, living a life that is ruled by what might go wrong, or might fail, or might be taken away.

Too much of your energy, and the energy you both draw from your environment and give back to it, will be destructive. Remember, your life is an ongoing creation, not a competition; there is no win or lose, but lessons; some you learn straight away, and some take a bit more time to grasp. Creating a new life or new opportunities is about holding that vision and then making it happen one step at a time. Be honest and realistic; otherwise, it may take much longer and much more energy to manifest what you want, and to be able to recognise what you need. Here are some tips to consider along the way:

> Exercise your experience. As an adult, you now have the mental and emotional maturity to delay or learn to delay gratification and to respond appropriately when things don't fall into place or go your way. Life has a habit of giving us what we need eventually, so don't get downcast or lose your temper if, at first, you don't succeed.

> Alter your attitude. If you get into the mindset of thinking the world owes you a living, then stop and consider how on earth you can be an effective creator if you are always waiting for something or someone else to do it for you or make it happen for you. Put in nothing, and you will get out of it even less. Feelings of entitlement or playing the victim are more likely to push away the very things and people you want in your life.

> Remove resentments. You could well experience ill feelings toward your parents, partners, peers, children, and friends. But harbouring resentments takes up

too much energy and time, and prevents you from functioning properly. By choosing to release your feelings of resentment, you will elevate your mood and regain time and energy for creating anew.

Swap negativity for gratitude. From time to time, you can get trapped in negative thoughts and just feed more of the same. If you feel helpless and hopeless more often than not, talk to someone who can help. Instead of looking at all that is wrong or lacking in your life, turn your focus to gratitude for what you have. Taking the time to remember what you have instead of fretting about what you think you are missing out on or do not have, changes your perspective for the better.

Preparation is key. Whether you are a list maker, lay out your clothes for the following day, prepare meals in advance, or actively set aside time to do things or meet people, you allow the subconscious to mentally work on things while you physically rest. And as people are generally creatures of habit, if you too can prepare well and get into good habits, such as getting regular exercise, you will feel better physically and emotionally. All this also helps you regain control over your life.

Don't ignore your emotions but do remember that feelings are not facts. Emotions need to be honoured, not justified, so even though you may have strong feelings about something, it does not make you right or your point any more valid than another's.

Know and honour who you really are. There is a saying, "fake it till you make it"; well, that's okay for some people sometimes, but it is much easier and more rewarding to be as authentic as you can, whenever you can. When you create, make plans, and build relationships based on truth, the foundations are solid, and you never need to "remember" what you said before. This way, you need not compromise your values or pretend to be someone you are not.

Your life is for living, so enjoy it. Start with taking pleasure out of the small things you do and achieve. Look out for the rays of sunshine that happen so often, but may go undetected. Make a point of seeing or saying something positive every day, complimenting a stranger, or just smiling more. You will soon notice the difference in projecting such positive energy on you, others, and the world you inhabit.

As creators, we are also creatures of connection. By that, I mean we like to form and maintain relationships with others, and it is also so valuable and important to connect to ourselves, both spiritually and physically. Our sense of "touch" is instrumental in maintaining healthy, strong bonds. That's why expressions such as "keeping in touch" or to "get a real feel for something" are so telling. Therefore, you could argue that Gaia as the goddess of ancient Greece or the planetary hypothesis put forward by Lovelock can seem a little out of reach to us as one individual. But, as I have said, this goddess is each of us and all of us, and versions of her are present throughout the world. And it is to one of these other versions that we now turn to demonstrate how Gaia can really become a tangible part of your life on a daily basis: a part that can be held, nurtured, and respected, a direct way of caring for your sacred self.

Many indigenous peoples of the Andes still revere Gaia today as "Pachamama," the Mother of Earth and time itself. She is seen as an ever-present and independent deity, wielding her own creative power to sustain life on this earth, and whose many shrines on earth consist of hollows in sacred trees and constructs of hallowed rocks. The four cosmological Quechua principles of Water, Earth, Sun, and Moon claim Pachamama as their creative source. Even after the Spanish colonised the Americas and converted native peoples to Roman Catholicism, Pachamama lived on through the Virgin Mary figure. And to this day, Pachamama is still believed to be a benevolent force, generous with her gifts, and intertwined as firmly as ever with the natural environment and environmental concerns. It is not hard to believe that our environment is suffering because people take too much from Pachamama.

This feeling of being stripped bare, of being taken advantage of, will occur within you from time to time also. This can be pretty valid, because someone is knowingly taking what they can from you; or inadvertently, when you allow people to take from you your time, energy, or material things beyond the point of comfort. In both instances, you have the ability to change it and restore your own balance, much in the same way our Gaia, Pachamama, or Mother Earth continuously battles to maintain a healthy environment for all life. You have to make your voice heard; that is a fundamental part of successfully journeying through your life and bearing the fruits of your creation. Gaia cannot speak to us directly. Instead, our environment's imbalances are highlighted via extreme weather patterns, earthquakes, and extinction events, in the hope that we will wake up to the signs and change our ways.

Your words and actions can be so powerful as to make people stop to look at their behaviour and change their ways; the key is always to do this in a measured way appropriate to the offending action. You would speak very differently to a fully aware person of the advantage they take of you than to one who has no idea. In this way, your energy is not unnecessarily exhausted, and hopefully, you don't lose your cool either. But when you have to deal with others' constant demands and impacts, it is too easy to lose sight of yourself and your needs. So I would like to introduce you to a very special creation, of your own making, that dates back to our indigenous ancestors' time and connects you to the essence of who you are; it is a "medicine bundle."

All wrapped up

A "medicine bundle" spiritually represents the person who creates it. They and similar items such as medicine bags and birthing bundles were first created for guidance, healing, and protection. The first time I ever encountered one was about fifteen years ago, when I had the privilege of spending time with Eliana Harvey, the founder of "Shamanka," a traditional school of women's shamanism in the United Kingdom. I had been chatting with Eliana about her journey to creating this fantastic facility when, out of the blue, she asked me about my path. I had always been curious about my existence. With the many opportunities for travel as a child and young woman, I told her I was now drawn to gathering and distributing whatever came my way, basically passing on information.

I was so struck by our journey's similarities and completely failed to notice Eliana retrieving a blanketed bundle in the shape of a parcel. "Would you like to hold this and tell me what you feel?" she said, carefully passing me this bundle with a soft smile on her face. Without any idea of what I was holding, I cradled the bundle that felt alive to me. It was warm and heavy, I shut my eyes, and I could see a baby inside this bundle; I could feel its head and bottom, and I wanted to rock it. I felt profound love wash over me. Eliana awaited my response. "I know this sounds silly, but I feel like I am holding a baby or small child, and I want to hold it—it is alive," I smiled. Eliana glowed as she said, "It is a birthing blanket; inside are rocks of my emotional being. I feel the same way as you do. It heals me. I sit with it against my back or hold it in my lap, and it soothes pain." I felt so very honoured that she had allowed me to spend time with her precious cargo. She went on to discuss "medicine bundles" in general: how they can be used to help people, to offer comfort and connection. Having held Eliana's bundle, I felt the sense of the life force these bundles can offer us and of their significance in our lives.

Eliana's birthing bundle is just one example of what you can create for yourself using earth-centred medicine. Your medicine bundle is sacred to you and should never be opened by anyone else. It contains items precious to you, things that offer comfort, protection, healing and connection to ancestors, goddesses, guides, angels, or power animals, whatever speaks to your heart. These items could be stones, figurines, dried herbs, a lock of hair, a crystal, a photo, a childhood toy, an item that represents a particular colour of meaning to you, and so on. Think of how each item represents your power to heal, guide, and protect yourself and gives you the strength to offer those things to others. This is your connection to your spiritual, creative essence.

◎ MAKING YOUR MEDICINE BUNDLE

Creating and having a medicine bundle has the capacity to increase your awareness of your own sacredness, the energy of the goddess within you. As you go through life, you may find other things you want to add to this bundle. In this way, it becomes like a manifestation of your energetic, spiritual self, who you really are, and something incredible to hand down to grandchildren who will respect its value. The medicine bundle that I invite you to create is based on the tradition of the peoples of the Americas, where medicine bundles are most commonly used.

YOU WILL NEED:

* A small handheld bell for cleansing
* Cloth for the outside cover, and an inner cloth, to form the lining (about 30 inches square for both)
* Cord, rope, or natural fibre twine to secure your bundle
* A small quartz crystal to heal and connect you to your spiritual self
* A few objects as a sacred representation of you

Begin making your medicine bundle by gathering all the materials together either on a table or on the floor before you. Now take your bell and proceed by "cleansing" the objects in front of you. To do this, take the bell or rattle in your dominant hand and ring/rattle as you move the tool in three circles over the items, then continue the cleansing by crossing over the items; first in a line straight ahead of you, northwards, back towards yourself, southwards, then back to the centre, then to your right, eastwards, then back to the centre, then to your left, west, westwards and complete the cross coming back to the centre of the space and stop. Put your cleansing tool down to one side.

Next, carefully gather up the material for the bundle's outer wrapping and the fabric for the bundle's lining. The outer fabric, known as "mesa," represents how you want to be seen by the outside world and project yourself to the world. This material is both sacred and symbolic. Choose a thicker, sturdy material that will wear well. Select the colour or pattern that means something to you. You can also embellish this as much as you like, sewing on whatever you wish to make it unique to you; some people might embellish it with beads or tassels or fringing of some kind, for example.

Now take the material that will act as the lining. This represents your inner world, what's underneath and not on display to the world unless you choose for it to be. This inner cloth will come into contact with your sacred items that will make up the contents of your bundle, which in turn will be wrapped and covered by the outer cloth. This lining should be of a far softer, more tactile material, like silk, fleece, or soft cotton. Now lay the lining on top of the outer cloth's inside to be perfectly aligned and pressed flat.

Now, take your sacred items in your dominant hand, one at a time. As you hold each object in your hand, close your eyes and take three deep breaths. Sense how the item feels in your hand; is it hot or cold, rough or smooth, heavy or light? Allow yourself a few moments to reminisce about what this object means to you or what it represents to you. Allow the positive feelings it invokes to wash over you once again, then open your eyes and place it gently and carefully onto the cloth in front of you. Finally, take the quartz crystal, hold it in your dominant hand and say, *Blessed be the contents of my bundle, thank you Mother Earth for their provision,* then place the crystal carefully amongst your sacred items. The essence of these particular items creates an energy in your medicine bundle, and that energy is the force that represents you.

Very carefully cover your medicine bundle contents with the soft lining material, and be sure they are well covered. When you are totally satisfied, take the outer fabric and wrap it snugly around the bundle; take great care that it only comes into contact with the lining and not the objects inside. Take the cord or rope you have picked out and secure your bundle. Do this by gathering all the material together from each corner to secure at the top (ensure to tuck in the lining first) by binding the cord around the "neck" of the gathered material. Or use a parcelling method, folding the lining so the parcel forms a square shape and you wrap the cord around from top to bottom and then from side to side, like dividing the parcel into quarters.

Now you have a very special "bundle" that you can have in your presence whenever you desire emotional healing, stability, protection, or reconnection with your goddess energy and creative power. Sit with it for a while and sense it: how it feels in your lap, the weight of it, how the items move inside as you breathe or when you hold it in your hands. Treat it with care as you would a living thing. You may want to share it with another person, allowing them to sit with it, and that is fine so long as it is only ever opened by you. Keep it in a safe place and visit with it often. Remember that you may want to add something to it or change the contents; just be sure each time to "cleanse" the items and follow the practice of bundling it up again with compassion and respect.

Born Again Creator, Resolution Tips

If everything is energy, and it is all universal energy, then we are all universally connected. But we are not all identical. Just as the same energy has come together to form mountains and lakes, animals and plants, you and everyone else on the planet, there are probably limitless "creations" that are still to come into being. You also have this within you, the ability to bring into being a myriad of feelings, talents, relationships, works of art, stories, poetry, or songs, and so much more. Until you are no longer on this Earth, opportunities exist for you to use your energy and your emotions to make your experience of this life as interesting, joyous, and fulfilling as you wish. Only you can do your best, and though you cannot control the people around you, just as Gaia cannot control us, how you respond to others and your environment goes a long way to making your path along this life one full of surprising deviations rather than a path of dead ends and pitfalls, so remember:

Coming to understand the difference between actual voids in your life that long to be filled and space that allows you time and energy to take a deep breath and reflect helps us to come to term with the concept of "doing nothing" and just being, as well as validating our desire to create something worthy.

Freely applying your inner potential, having healthier relationships, more fulfilment in your job, and greater control of your emotional state comes with practice.

Consider the context of what it means to be "all as one" from a numerological understanding and from a holistic perspective. This will help to understand the feeling of being whole, just as you are.

Gaia is the life-giver and the energy that fills the great void of Chaos to enrich our universe. If the universe was a sacred orchestra playing, Gaia would be the conductor and all the instruments, and you would be the music that is made. Make yourself heard!

Communing with Gaia is something we do all the time, simply by being alive; we breathe air, bask in the sunshine, walk in the countryside, and so on. Practising "attunement" is a wonderful way to actively re-engage with Gaia by focusing our attention and awareness on the world around us and its ties to our very existence.

Your creation story is about being actively engaged in your life, taking responsibility for what you say and do and how you express your feelings and act upon them. You can do this successfully, i.e., with the least amount of resistance, by remembering to exercise your experience, alter your attitude, remove resentments, swap negativity for gratitude, prepare, acknowledge your emotions, know and honour who you really are, and above all, enjoy your life.

Pachamama is the personification of our natural environment directly related to the impact of our behaviour on this planet that works so hard to sustain life as we know it. Relating that to a "mother" deity, we can feel empathy and compassion for what we are doing to "her" that either causes upset or can heal.

You are not just a person of the mind but also of the body and the spirit. Your medicine bundle can help you to tangibly connect with all aspects of who you are now, the experiences that got you to this place, and give you comfort and inspiration that you have what it takes to navigate your way into a future of your creation.

Conclusion

You are here for a reason, not some "saviour complex" type of reason, but because incredible, non-judgemental, vibrant universal energy came into being through your existence. You are the stuff of stars, and you can create as much or as little as you choose, so by choosing to create now with a clearer head and a compassionate heart, then stronger relationships, a more fulfilling outlook, and a healthier planet will be just some of your rewards. Being the ultimate creator in your life does not mean that you now have all the answers or that you can manage everything and anything in your life without batting an eyelid. You are still the complex, emotionally driven you, but I hope what you are coming to realise is that you have support, help, and options in life. Managing your emotional triggers is half the battle to creating circumstances in life that are more neutral or productive than destructive.

How you now respond to your environment will determine what is to come. By re-engaging with your goddess energy, and understanding your emotional responses, you can adapt where and when necessary. The simple act of taking time for yourself to breathe deeply, or be in nature, or state your intention is of immense benefit. Without you even thinking about it, it changes your energy and physiology for the better. Your expectations might be that your life is revolutionised by what you have read and done. It may not be immediately apparent, but if you take these ideas and practices with you into your daily life, change will happen.

Practice, and be patient, for if any of these things are new to you, you will not master them immediately, and that is perfectly okay; they will have an effect long before you master them anyway. And remember all the tools at our disposal, which include conventional medicines and therapies, one of the best being the ability to talk and listen. Remember you are the storyteller of your life, that how you feel has the most significant influence on how you experience this life. Through your experiences, trials, and triumphs, you can positively affect others. Don't hold back; live, love, and create!

Acknowledgements

To my wonderful family: thank you for giving me the space to do what I love without question. Thank you for showing me so much of the world and so much of myself and loving me through it all.

To a trio of extraordinary friends, Sarah, Dawn, and Julia: you are all goddesses in my eyes; thank you for being there, in times of laughter and times of tears. Remember how beautiful and unique you all are.

To Barbara Meiklejohn-Free: I give thanks for your friendship, inspiration, and encouragement to take risks and rejoice in the mystery of life.

To all my brilliant clients, especially Stephanie, Flavia, and Claire, from whom I have learned so much: may your work go on to help and inspire all who need it in their lives.

To Bill and Heather from Llewellyn: thank you for your belief in my work, for taking risks, and for your support in all its guises.

To Eliana Harvey: thank you for your foreword and all the work you have done over the years to support women along the shamanic path.

To all my friends, past and present: my journey has been made all the richer because of knowing you, and for that, I am so grateful.

Further Reading

Great Goddesses: Life Lessons from Myths and Monsters, by Nikita Gill, Ebury Press (2019)

Classical Mythology A to Z: An Encyclopedia of Gods & Goddesses, Heroes & Heroines, Nymphs, Spirits, Monsters, and Places, by Annette Giesecke, Black Dog & Leventhal (2020)

Wicca Magical Deities: A Guide to the Wiccan God and Goddess, and Choosing a Deity to Work Magic With, by Lisa Chamberlain, CreateSpace Independent Publishing Platform (2016)

The Great Goddess: Reverence of the Divine Feminine from the Paleolithic to the Present, by Jean Markale, Inner Traditions Bear and Company (2000)

The Living Goddesses, by Marija Gimbutas, University of California Press (2001)

Great Cosmic Mother: Rediscovering the Religion of the Earth, by Monica Sjoo & Barbara Mor, Bravo Ltd. (1991)

Orishas, Goddesses, and Voodoo Queens: The Divine Feminine in the African Religious Traditions, by Lilith Dorsey, Weiser Books (2020)

When Women Ruled the World: Six Queens of Egypt Hardcover, by Kara Cooney, National Geographic (2018)

Keeping Her Keys: An Introduction to Hekate's Modern Witchcraft, by Cyndi Brannen, Moon Books (2019)

Dark Goddess Oracle Cards, F.K. Peters, B. Meiklejohn-Free, and K. Osborne, Llewellyn Publications (2018)

Bibliography

Aurelius, Marcus. *Meditations*. Penguin Books Ltd, 2006.

Browder, Anthony T. *Nile Valley Contributions to Civilization*. Institute of Karmic Guidance, 1992.

Black Koltuv, Barbara. *The Book of Lilith*. Nicolas-Hays, Inc., 1986.

Brennan, Barbara A. *Hands of Light: A Guide to Healing Through the Human Energy Field*. Bantam, 1988.

Brown, Robert G. *The Book of Lilith*. Lulu.com, 2007.

Bruce, Robert. *Energy Work: The Secrets of Healing and Spiritual Growth*. Hampton Roads Publishing, 2011.

Chinnaiyan, Kavitha M. *Shakti Rising: Embracing Shadow and Light on the Goddess Path to Wholeness*. Non-Duality, 2017.

Easwaran, Eknath. *The Upanishads*. Nilgiri Press, 1987.

Gimbutas, Marija. *The Civilization of the Goddess: The World of Old Europe*. HarperSanFrancisco, 1991.

Hall, Judy. *The Crystal Bible*. Krause Publications, 2003.

Hancock, Graham. *Fingerprints of The Gods: The Quest Continues*. Century, 2001.

Hesiod, and M. L. West. *Theogony and Works and Days*. Oxford University Press, 2009.

Jung, Carl G. *Memories, Dreams, Reflections*. Vintage Books USA, 1989.

Lovelock, James. *The Ages of Gaia: A Biography of Our Living Earth*. W. W. Norton & Co. 1995.

MacLaine, Shirley. *Sage-ing while Age-ing*. Simon & Schuster UK Ltd, 2007.

Mallon, Brenda. *The Mystic Symbols: A Complete Guide to Magic and Sacred Signs and Symbols*. Godsfield Press, 2007.

Markale, Jean. *The Great Goddess: Reverence of the Divine Feminine from the Paleolithic to the Present*. Inner Traditions, 1999.

Meadows, Kenneth. *Earth Medicine: A Shamanic Way to Self Discovery*. Element Books Ltd, 1989.

Meiklejohn-Free, Barbara. *Scottish Witchcraft: A Complete Guide to Authentic Folklore, Spells and Magickal Tools*. Llewellyn Worldwide Ltd, 2019.

Meiklejohn-Free, Barbara. *The Shaman Within: Reclaiming our Rites of Passage*. Moon Books, 2013

Miller, Patricia L. and Wayne K. Powell. *Hawaiian Shamanistic Healing: Medicine Ways to Cultivate the Aloha Spirit*. Llewellyn Publications, 2018.

Mountford, Charles P. *The Dreamtime: Australian Aboriginal Myths*. Robert Hale & Company, 1974.

Nelson, Dr. Bradley. *The Emotion Code: How to Release Your Trapped Emotions for Abundant Health, Love, and Happiness.* St. Martin's Essentials, 2019.

Orr, Leonard. *Breaking the Death Habit: The Science of Everlasting Life.* North Atlantic Books, 1998.

Oschman, James L. *Energy Medicine: The Scientific Basis.* Churchill Livingstone, 2000.

Peck Scott, M. *The Road Less Travelled: The Classic Work on Relationships, Spiritual Growth and Life's Meaning.* Rider, 2008.

Peters, Flavia K., B. Meiklejohn-Free, and K. Osborne. *Dark Goddess Oracle Cards.* Llewellyn Worldwide Ltd, 2018.

Phillips, David. *The Complete Book of Numerology.* Hay House Inc., 2005.

Pierre, Wolff. *Discernment: The Art of Choosing Well.* Liguori; Rev ed. Edition, 2003.

Skinner, Stephen. *Sacred Geometry: Deciphering the Code.* Gaia Books, 2006.

Woodfield, Stephanie. *Dark Goddess Craft: A Journey through the Heart of Transformation.* Llewellyn Publications, 2017.

To Write to the Author

If you wish to contact the author or would like more information about this book, please write to the author in care of Llewellyn Worldwide Ltd. and we will forward your request. Both the author and publisher appreciate hearing from you and learning of your enjoyment of this book and how it has helped you. Llewellyn Worldwide Ltd. cannot guarantee that every letter written to the author can be answered, but all will be forwarded. Please write to:

Kate Osborne
⅏ Llewellyn Worldwide
2143 Wooddale Drive
Woodbury, MN 55125-2989
Please enclose a self-addressed stamped envelope for reply,
or $1.00 to cover costs. If outside the U.S.A., enclose
an international postal reply coupon.

Many of Llewellyn's authors have websites with additional information and resources. For more information, please visit our website at http://www.llewellyn.com.